Understanding
Jesus

Understanding Jesus

Who Jesus Christ Is and Why He Matters

ALISTER MCGRATH

Academie Books
Grand Rapids, Michigan
Zondervan Publishing House

UNDERSTANDING JESUS
Copyright © 1987 by Alister McGrath

ACADEMIE BOOKS is an imprint of Zondervan Publishing House,
1415 Lake Drive, S.E., Grand Rapids, Michigan 49506.

Library of Congress Cataloging in Publication Data
McGrath, Alister E., 1953-
    Understanding Jesus.

    "Academie books."
    1. Jesus Christ—Person and offices. I. Title.
BT202.M398   1987   232   87-6257
ISBN 0-310-29810-5

Biblical quotations are from the Revised Standard Version, copyrighted
1946, 1952 © 1971, 1973 by the Division of Christian Education of the
National Council of the Churches of Christ in the USA.

Printed in the United States of America

87 88 89 90 91 92 93 / AH / 10 9 8 7 6 5 4 3 2 1

For Paul

Contents

Foreword

One very great weakness in contemporary Christianity is this: competent communicators of the faith are not very numerous, and are not usually very learned. Those who give their lives to the study of these great truths are often very indifferent communicators. It is rarely that you find a man with great erudition who has the ability to distil it in terms which anyone can understand. Alister McGrath is such a man. He is quite brilliant. He got his First in theology at Oxford, while at the same time completing his doctorate in molecular biology! He is one of the major international experts on Luther. He teaches theology at Oxford. And yet he is able to teach total beginners, in language that is clear and untechnical. He is able to write, as he does in this book, on great themes without using long words and heavy footnotes.

So I welcome this book most enthusiastically. It is an excellent example of profundity married to simplicity. And I am sure that Dr McGrath will write a lot more in this vein, to the great benefit of the general Christian public, as well as producing the major theological works for which he is so well equipped.

But I welcome the book for another reason. England is not a land which breeds systematic theologians. Maybe that is not altogether a bad thing, because no mortal man can get

God systematized! But the shortage in systematic theology in this country means that it is not easy for the non-expert to find a book which explains to him clearly and intelligently who Jesus is and what he has done for us. Within the pages of this book you will find a careful, well-argued explanation of the evidence about Jesus, the nature and purpose of the gospels, and why it is important to reach clear views about Jesus. You will then be led into a most illuminating investigation of Jesus' person and work, embracing the central tenets of the Christian faith: the incarnation, the cross and the resurrection. It is a splendid guide through the complexities of these vital doctrines. And it will surely encourage many a reader to go further in his investigations. But above all it gives to the believer a clear reason for the Christian faith which is within him, and to the enquirer a clear understanding of what Christians believe, and why.

I am excited by this book, and shall be surprised if you are not, too!

MICHAEL GREEN

Introduction

Christianity has much to say about God and about man. It claims to possess certain crucial insights into the character and purposes of God, and the nature and ultimate destiny of man. It makes claims concerning the meaning of life, and the significance of death. What is particularly distinctive about Christianity, however, is not just these crucial insights themselves, but the way in which we come to know about them in the first place. The Christian faith is ultimately based upon the person of Jesus Christ. Just as a lens may focus the complex elements of a picture into a single point of light, so the many elements of the Christian faith are focused upon the single historical person of Jesus Christ. Who is Jesus Christ? And why is he so important? The Christian understanding of God and man arises from the Christian understanding of the *identity* and *significance* of Jesus Christ. In this sense, Jesus Christ may be said to be the foundation, the centre, the focus and the heart of the Christian faith.

This work is simply an attempt to explain the Christian understanding of the identity and significance of Jesus Christ, and its consequences.

PART 1
Getting Started

1

Jesus and Christianity

One of the greatest mysteries of life is why some lectures are unspeakably tedious, and others spellbinding. Late in 1899, a series of lectures was given at the University of Berlin by an elderly professor of church history. His subject – the nature of Christianity. His audience – students drawn from every faculty in the university. The lectures were a sensation. Perhaps it was on account of his subject; perhaps it was the fact that the lectures were delivered completely without notes, so that they would have been lost for ever were it not for one thoughtful member of his audience who jotted them down in shorthand as they were delivered. The opening sentences of those lectures are memorable:

> The great English philosopher, John Stuart Mill, somewhere observed that mankind cannot be reminded too often that there was once a man whose name was Socrates. That is true – but it is still more important to remind mankind again and again that a man whose name was Jesus Christ once stood in their midst.

At the heart of the Christian faith lies not so much a set of abstract ideas or beliefs but a person. We must resist the temptation to speak about Christianity as if it were some form of 'ism', like Marxism, Darwinism or Hegelianism. These are essentially abstract systems which have become detached from the person of their founder, and reduced

15

simply to sets of doctrines. Although the ideas which we call 'Marxism' were originally developed by Marx, the ideas are now quite independent of him. All that Marx did was to introduce them. The relationship between Jesus and Christianity is, however, quite different.

Christians have always insisted that there was something special, something qualitatively different, about Jesus which sets him apart from religious teachers or thinkers, and demands careful consideration. There is a close connection between the person and the message of Jesus – and if anything, it is Jesus' person – what he did, and the impact he made on those who encountered him – which make his message important. From the outset, Christians appear to have realized that Jesus just could not be treated as an ordinary mortal. As we shall see later, from the earliest of times Christians worshipped and adored Jesus as if he were God. While recognizing the difficulties – and even the dangers – of speaking in this way, the Christian will insist that, in a very real sense, Jesus is the whole of the gospel message; and that when he speaks of God, he actually means God as he has been revealed to us in the face of Jesus Christ.

In Jesus, the message and the messenger are one and the same. Jesus' message is given weight and status because of who we recognize Jesus to be. As we shall see later, the resurrection of Jesus appears to have been the decisive factor in forcing the first Christians to begin to take the astonishing – but to them necessary and appropriate – step of thinking of Jesus as God, in some sense of the word. We could put this more formally by saying that Jesus Christ is the object of faith, rather than just an example of faith. The challenge posed to every succeeding generation by the New Testament witness to Jesus is not so much, 'What did he teach?' but 'Who is he? And what is his relevance for us?' Christianity doesn't necessarily claim to possess all truth – but if it loses sight of its central conviction that in Christ it has found access to the deepest truths about God and man, it has lost itself.

The gospels tell us that as Jesus was walking with his disciples in the region of Caesarea Philippi, he suddenly asked them a question: 'Who do men say that I am?' The disciples replied with a variety of answers – they told him that some people thought that he was John the Baptist, others Elijah, Jeremiah or some other prophet. Jesus then asks his disciples the crucial question, which demands that they speak for themselves, instead of merely reporting the opinions of others. 'Who do *you* say that I am?' And Peter replied for them all when he answered: 'You are the Christ, the Son of the living God' (Matthew 16:13–16). The central challenge posed to the reader of the New Testament, especially the four gospels, concerns the identity and relevance of Jesus Christ.

'Who do *you* say that I am?' As we read the gospels, it is impossible to avoid the impression that we have met a real person. There are many historical characters whom we may know much about – for example, Alexander the Great, Julius Caesar or Admiral Nelson – yet who fail to make a personal impression upon us. They remain figures from the past, whom we do not feel we know by personal acquaintance. Equally, there are many fictional characters who never existed in reality, and yet we feel we 'know' them as real people – obvious examples might be Shakespeare's Falstaff, Mr Pickwick, or Sherlock Holmes.

There are surprisingly few actual historical figures who come over as personalities – people whom we can know personally. An obvious example is Dr Samuel Johnson, as recorded for us by Boswell, who comes across as a rather grave and melancholy figure who still has a love of fun and nonsense ('The Irish are a fair people – they never speak well of one another'). Another is Socrates, as we find him in Plato's dialogues. But the most important of all is the Jesus we encounter in the gospel narratives.

Although an historical figure who lived and died in an obscure and uninteresting part of the world two thousand

years ago, he comes across as someone we feel we know in
the same sense as we know a real and living person – someone whom we can *know*, rather than just *know about*. One
of his more reluctant and sceptical admirers once wrote: 'We
know no-one as well as we know Jesus.' For precisely this
reason, the figure of Jesus Christ exercises a remarkable
influence over many who would not dream of regarding
themselves as Christians. But what is it about Jesus that
causes him to exercise such a remarkable and pervasive
influence over men and women some two thousand years
after his birth? And how can we make sense of his identity
and significance? It is with the unfolding and answering of
these questions that this book is concerned.

Who is Jesus Christ? Our first attempt to answer this
question might go something like this: Jesus was a first-
century Jew who lived in Palestine in the reign of Tiberius
Caesar and was executed by crucifixion under Pontius Pilate.
The Roman historian Tacitus refers to Christians deriving
their name from 'Christ, who was executed at the hands
of the procurator Pontius Pilate in the reign of Tiberius'
(*Annals*, xv, 44, 3).

The historical evidence for his existence is sufficient to
satisfy all but those who are determined to believe that he
didn't exist, whatever the evidence may be. Indeed, if the
existence of Jesus is denied, despite all the evidence we
possess which points to the opposite conclusion, consistency
would demand that we deny the existence of an alarming
number of historical figures, the evidence for whose existence is considerably more slender than that of Jesus.

The historical evidence we possess concerning the origins
of Christianity and the character of its early beliefs is most
easily explained on the basis of the existence of Jesus as a
real historical figure. It involves the most tortuous explanation if he did not exist. Indeed, if Jesus did not exist as an
historical figure it would probably be necessary to suppose
that someone remarkably like him did in order to explain the

evidence in our possession. Thus St Paul takes Jesus' existence as a fact which does not require demonstration, and concentrates upon establishing and defending the significance of his life, death and resurrection.

That Jesus did *not* exist is a dogmatic presupposition quite unacceptable to the unbiased historian, rather than an obvious – or even plausible – conclusion of a detailed study of the evidence. Although there have been, and almost certainly always will be, those who argue that Jesus did not exist, and although they will doubtless continue to provide straws to be grasped by those determined to disprove Christianity, the fact remains that they are simply not taken seriously by disinterested and impartial historical scholarship.

So far, so good. What of the evidence that Jesus was crucified under the procurator Pontius Pilate? One of the earliest literary witnesses to this fact is Paul's first letter to the Christian church at Corinth, probably dating from the early months of A.D. 54. In the first chapter of this letter, Paul lays considerable emphasis upon the fact that Christ was crucified. The subject of his preaching was 'Christ crucified' (v. 23); the power lying behind the gospel proclamation is 'the cross of Christ' (v. 17); the entire gospel can even be summarized as 'the word of the cross' (v. 18). If the tradition concerning the crucifixion of Jesus was an invention of the first Christians, we can only conclude that it demonstrates that they were too stupid for words, as the idea of a crucified saviour was immediately seized upon by the opponents of the early church as an absurdity, demonstrating the ridiculous nature of Christian claims.

Justin Martyr, attempting to defend Christianity against its more sophisticated critics in the second century, conceded that the Christian proclamation of a crucified Christ appeared to be madness:

> [The opponents of Christianity] say that our madness lies in the fact that we put a crucified man in second place to the unchangeable and eternal God, the creator of the world (*Apology* I, xiii, 4).

For a Jew, anyone hanged upon a tree was to be regarded as cursed by God (Deuteronomy 21:23), which would hardly commend the Christian claim that Jesus was indeed the long-awaited Messiah. Indeed, one of the Dead Sea scrolls suggests that crucifixion was regarded as the proper form of execution for a Jew suspected of high treason.

It is clear from contemporary evidence that crucifixion was a widespread form of execution within the Roman Empire, and that there was an astonishing variety of manners in which this execution might be carried out. It is impossible to define what form a 'normal' crucifixion might take. The victim was generally flogged or tortured beforehand, and then might be tied or nailed to the cross in practically any position, subject only to the ingenuity and perversity of the executioner. Far from being an essentially bloodless form of execution, as some commentators have suggested, the victim would have bled profusely. Only if he had not been flogged or tortured previously, and bound, rather than nailed, to the cross, would no blood have been spilled.

The punishment appears to have been employed particularly in the suppression of rebellious provincials, such as the Cantabrians in northern Spain, as well as the Jews. Josephus' accounts of the crucifixion of countless Jewish fugitives who attempted to escape from besieged Jerusalem make horrifying reading. In the view of most Roman jurists, notorious criminals should be crucified on the exact location of their crime, so that 'the sight may deter others from such crimes'. Perhaps for this reason, Quintillian crucified criminals on the busiest thoroughfares in order that the maximum deterrent effect might be acheived.

It is therefore small wonder that the pagan world of the first century reacted with disbelief or disgust to the Christians' suggestion that they should take seriously 'an evil man and his cross' (*homo noxius et crux eius*) to the point of worshipping him. Crucifixion was a punishment reserved for the lowest criminals, clearly implying that Jesus was one of their number. Jesus 'endured the cross, despising the shame' (Hebrews 12:2). The tradition of the crucifixion of Jesus Christ is deeply embedded in the New Testament witness to him at every level. It is impossible to account for this unless it is based upon an historical fact. If the early Christians had based their message upon a fictitious figure or upon a real figure whom they deliberately misrepresented, they would have been fools to portray Jesus as having been *crucified*. Nothing could have been calculated to have evoked a more universal negative reaction on the part of their audience as the early Christians proclaimed the gospel. Were the first Christians *really* that stupid? Would they have invented such a story, which could only be used against them? Once more, there is no reason for any except a dogmatic critic, who is determined to disbelieve each and every statement made by the New Testament concerning Jesus as a matter of principle, to call into question the historical nature of the crucifixion of Jesus.

But it is at this point that we must pause to reflect. The Christian faith certainly presupposes that Jesus existed as a real historical figure and that he was crucified. Christianity is, however, most emphatically not *about* the mere facts that Jesus existed and was crucified. Let us recall some words of Paul:

> Now I would remind you, brethren, in what terms I preached to you the gospel, which you received, in which you stand, by which you are saved, if you hold it fast – unless you believed in vain. For I delivered to you as of first importance what I also received, that Christ died for our sins in accordance with the scriptures, that he was buried, that he was raised on the third day in accordance with the scriptures, and that he appeared to Cephas [Peter], then to the twelve [apostles] (1 Corinthians 15:1–5).

The use of the words 'delivered' and 'received' is very important. They are drawn from the technical language of tradition, of 'handing down', and point to the fact that Paul is passing on to his readers something that had earlier been passed on to him. In other words, Paul was not the first to summarize the Christian faith in terms of these two essential components (Jesus' crucifixion and resurrection) – he had learned this from others. Paul is not relying here on his own memory, but on the collective memory of a much larger group of people. It is widely believed that Paul is reciting a formula, a form of words, which was in general use in the early church and which he himself had received – not just in general terms but in almost exactly the same form as he passes it down to the Corinthian Christians. He is relying not on his own memory but on that of the Christian church in the earliest period of its existence.

Earlier in this letter, Paul had made it clear that the content of his preaching to the Corinthian Christians, upon which their faith was based, was 'Christ crucified' (1:17–18; 2:2). It is now clear that two important points must be noted. First, Paul affirms that the Christ who died upon the cross was raised again from the dead. Secondly, Paul states that not only did Christ *die*, he *died for our sins*. We shall consider each of these two points separately.

Concerning the first of these points, the historical event of the crucifixion was followed by that of the resurrection, and Paul's exposition of the significance of Jesus Christ for mankind is based upon these two events being linked. But whereas it was commonplace for men to be crucified at that time, we possess no account of any other crucified individual being raised from the dead. Indeed, there appears to have been no other case of resurrection in the course of human history. This has prompted some critics to suggest that the event never, in fact, took place. We shall consider this suggestion in chapter four. But it is notable that Paul links Jesus' death and resurrection together as the two elements of his gospel. Jesus 'was put to death for our trespasses and raised for our justification' (Romans 4:25).

Secondly, Paul makes a clear distinction between the *event* of the death of Christ, and the *significance* of this event. That

Christ died is a simple matter of history; that Christ died *for our sins* is the gospel itself. Even if it could be demonstrated to the satisfaction of the most biased opponent of Christianity that Jesus Christ really did exist, and that he died upon a cross, this would not prove the truth of the Christian faith. The Christian faith is based upon certain historical events, but is not to be identified with those events alone; rather, it is to be identified with an *interpretation* of these events.

The distinction between an *event* and its *meaning* must be appreciated. Let us take a well-known example. In 49 B.C. Julius Caesar crossed a small river with a single legion of men. The name of that river was the Rubicon, and it marked the boundary between Italy and Cisalpine Gaul. The political significance of that event was that it marked a declaration of war on the part of Caesar against Pompey and the Roman senate. The *event* was the crossing of a river; the *meaning* of that event was a declaration of war.

In many ways, the death of Christ may be said to parallel Caesar's crossing of the Rubicon. The event itself appears unexceptional except to those who know its significance. The Rubicon was a small river and it was not difficult to cross. People had crossed much wider rivers before and have done since then. As an *event* it hardly seems significant. Similarly, Jesus died upon a cross. Every man must die at some point. On the basis of contemporary records, we know that an incalculable number of people died in this way at that time. As an *event* it hardly seems important or noteworthy. On the other hand, those aware of the *meaning* of the event saw beyond it, to what it signified, to the reason why it was important. Pompey and the Roman senate were not interested in the mechanics of how Caesar crossed the Rubicon – for them it meant war. Similarly, Paul was not particularly interested in the mechanics of the crucifixion of Jesus – for him, it meant salvation, forgiveness and victory over death. Thus the 'word of the cross' was not concerned with the simple fact that Jesus was crucified, but with the significance of this event for man.

Every now and then books with titles like *Great Moments from English Literature* make their appearance. I think we can safely say that the following lines by Frederick Langbridge will not feature prominently in them!

> Two men look out through the same bars:
> One sees the mud, and one the stars.

It is quite possible for two observers to be in the same position, and yet see something quite different. In this case, Langbridge draws our attention to the fact that two men, looking out through the same prison bars, see very different things. One looks down and sees the mud; the other lifts his eyes to heaven and sees the stars. The point that Langbridge is trying to make is that some men see nothing but the rut of everyday life ending in death, while others raise their eyes to heaven knowing that their ultimate destiny lies with God. Their situation is identical – but their outlooks are totally different.

Much the same is true of the cross. Two observers may contemplate the cross. One observer may see nothing more than an everyday execution of an unimportant Jew; another may see the Saviour of the world dying for him. As we have tried to make clear, Christianity is not just about the *fact* of the cross – it is about realizing its full meaning. That Jesus died is a statement about an historical event – that Jesus died *for us* is a statement about the *meaning* of that event, and is nothing less than the gospel itself.

This point is so important it needs further discussion. We are not talking about two or more different ways of looking at the same thing. All of us are used to the fact that a painting which seems grotesque to one onlooker appears to be nothing less than inspired to another. Here the object is the same – what is different is that which is seen in it. The cross is somewhat different, and is better understood from the following illustration.

Let us suppose that two observers are standing on the white cliffs of Dover, at some point during the period 26th

May–3rd June 1940. They see lots of little boats coming and going from the local harbours. For one observer, all that is happening is a relatively unimportant event – the movement of boats. Another observer sees exactly the same events, but is aware of a deeper and more significant truth linked to those events which the other observer misses. He knows that the little boats are engaged in the evacuation of the British Expeditionary Force from Dunkirk in France, and that the success of the operation holds the key to further resistance to Hitler, upon which the outcome of the Second World War will ultimately depend.

Both observers see the same events; one recognizes the crucial significance of what he sees, whereas the other does not. One, knowing the background to what is going on and knowing of the desperate situation in France on account of the astonishingly rapid German advance, recognizes that he is witnessing a moment in history upon which much depends. The other sees nothing but the sea and some boats.

The same is true of the cross. The observer who knew the background, who knew of the mysterious prophecies of the suffering servant and who knew that Jesus had foretold his death, recognized the full meaning of the event. Let us go back to our Dunkirk illustration for a moment. One observer noticed nothing more than lots of boats moving about in the English Channel; another saw the salvation of what remained of the British Army and war effort. So it is with the cross. One observer might notice a man dying on a cross; another sees God working out in a mysterious manner the salvation of mankind.

The same sort of point could be made with reference to the parables. When Jesus told parables, all those listening heard exactly the same words. For example, all those around heard Jesus tell the parable of the Prodigal Son – a story about a boy who leaves home, only to return (Luke 15:11–32). Yet although everyone heard the same story, two quite different reactions to that story can be seen. Some heard a story about a boy who ran away from home, while others heard about the overwhelming and amazing love of God for sinful man. One group heard the story and missed its meaning; the other group heard exactly the same story and realized what it meant. For this second group the penny had dropped. So it is with the cross. To some it is just about the death of a man; to others it is about God entering into his world to redeem those whom he loved.

It is also important to appreciate that a careful distinction must be made between the *truth* and *relevance* of an event. An event may be true, and yet quite without relevance. There will be few who will find themselves even remotely excited by the fact that the capital of Albania is Tirana, or by the accuracy of the annual rainfall figures for the Scottish Highlands. The truth of an event alone is not sufficient to ensure its appeal or relevance. In fact, something may be quite *untrue* and enormously significant. For example, in the mid-1850s new rifles were issued to soldiers of the East India Company. The old 'Brown Bess' was replaced with the Enfield rifle which used a different type of cartridge. It was widely believed by the Indian sepoys that the Enfield cartridges were greased with beef fat (which would be defiling to a Hindu) or pig fat (which would be defiling to a Muslim). Although this rumour does not appear to have been based upon fact, it was sufficient to act as a major contributing cause to the Indian Mutiny of 1857. Although not true, it was certainly thought to be relevant!

It will be clear, however, that Paul is making two important statements concerning the crucifixion: first, it is *true*; secondly, it is *relevant*. In other words, the event of the crucifixion really took place and its significance is such that it has continuing relevance for man.

With this point in mind, let us return to the question of who Jesus is. The words of an early German Reformer (Philip Melanchthon) are worth noting here: 'To know Christ is to know his benefits.' We are actually dealing with two quite different yet closely related questions. One is the question of the *identity* of Jesus: who is he? The other is the question of the *function* of Jesus: what does he do? If we are going to assess the significance of Jesus, we have to deal with both these questions. Let us illustrate this point with some examples.

It is possible to argue from Jesus' function to his identity. The following argument was used extensively by the early church. First, it was stated that Jesus was the Saviour of the world, thus establishing his function (in other words, what he does – he saves). Secondly, it was argued that the only one who could save man was God. Therefore, if Jesus saved man he must be God. Beginning from Jesus' function, his identity was deduced.

Or the argument could be used the other way round – to work from Jesus' identity to his function. It would be argued that Jesus was God (which is a statement about his identity). Therefore, it is argued, Jesus must reveal God (which is a statement about his function).

For our purposes, it doesn't matter which way round this is argued. The point we want to make is that Jesus' identity and significance are closely related. In establishing who Jesus *is*, we have to bear in mind what he *does*. For Paul, Jesus was the bearer of salvation to sinful man. The 'benefits of Christ' were the forgiveness of sins, reconciliation to God, and the hope of resurrection. To 'know Christ' thus involves recognizing his significance for us – in other words, recognizing the 'benefits' which he brings, making them our own and subsequently reflecting upon who Jesus must be if he is able to do this for us.

Who is this man through whom the Christian church has always claimed that she has forgiveness of sins? Who is this man whom Christians have worshipped as if he were God? What is so special about this man's death that Christians *celebrate* it where mourning might seem more appropriate?

It is questions like these which come together under the general area of theology known as 'Christology', or 'the doctrine of the person and work of Christ', and which we shall be considering in the remainder of this book.

2

Why Have Doctrines about Jesus?

Theology is often regarded as idle and pointless speculation abut irrelevancies – a harmless, if somewhat pointless, pastime of frustrated academics and bishops with time on their hands. If any area of Christian thought has been characterized by apparently pointless speculation of this sort, it is Christology. Gregory of Nyssa, writing in the fourth century, complained that it was impossible to go out shopping in downtown Constantinople without having to put up with speculation of this sort:

> Constantinople is full of mechanics and slaves, every one of them profound theologians, who preach in the shops and streets. If you want someone to change a piece of silver, he tells you about how the Son differs from the Father; if you ask the price of a loaf of bread, you are told that the Son is inferior to the Father; if you ask whether the bath is ready, you are told that the Son was created from nothing.

There is a widespread feeling inside and outside the Christian church today – as there always has been and probably always will be – that doctrines and dogmas are a waste of time. The Christian creeds all too often appear as arid and dead formulas, bearing little relation to the faith of those who have to repeat them. The great Austrian philosopher Wittgenstein remarked that 'Christianity is not a doctrine, not, I mean, a theory about what has happened and what will

29

happen to the human soul, but a description of something that actually takes place in human life'. In other words, experience of God and Christ comes before doctrines about them.

The Christian who turns from his real and profound experience of God to the terse and bleak statements of the creeds of the church inevitably feels that they are petty, pedantic and unreal – totally incapable of capturing his experience or adequately reflecting it. How can the immensity, the richness, the vitality and the sheer wonder of the Christian's experience of God in Christ be expressed in such clumsy terms? Indeed, why bother with doctrines at all? It is this question which we must consider before going any further, because inevitably we are going to end up talking about doctrines concerning Jesus.

Christians are faced with something of a dilemma. On the one hand, they *want* to talk about God as the one whom they experience, love and worship in adoration and wonder. On the other, they are only too painfully aware of the simple fact that God is God, and human language is quite incapable of adequately expressing everything which they would want to say about him. The words of the psalmist are worth recalling: 'Be still, and know that I am God.' The majesty and wonder of God tends to reduce us to silence. But we *must* speak of God, despite recognizing the inadequacy of our words, to do justice either to God himself or even to our experience of him.

When I began to study theology at Oxford, one of my tutors was a Jesuit at Campion Hall. As I climbed the staircase leading to his room, I used to pass a gigantic painting of a man and a small boy by the sea. Eventually, I asked someone to explain the painting, and was told the following story. Once upon a time, Augustine of Hippo, a celebrated theologian, was writing a work on the Trinity, exploring the Christian understanding of God. As he was walking along the coast one day, he encountered a small boy pouring seawater into a hole in the ground. Augustine watched him for some time, and eventually asked him what he was doing. 'I'm pouring the Mediterranean Sea into this hole,' replied the boy.

'Don't be so stupid,' replied Augustine, 'you can't fit the sea into that little hole. You're wasting your time.'

'And so are you,' replied the boy, 'trying to write a book about God.' (It's one of those stories which, if it *isn't* true, certainly ought to be!)

But even with this sobering thought in mind, Augustine still felt it was important to try and speak about God – and inevitably to speak of him in terms of doctrines. In fact, it took centuries for the church to sort out the full significance of its experience of God and Christ and express it – rather clumsily – in the doctrine of the Trinity. But it will be obvious that the Christian experience of God, Christ and the Holy Spirit was something common to Christian experience long before it was expressed in words or doctrines or wrapped up in some sort of doctrinal formula.

In turning from our experience of God or Jesus to doctrines about them, we are inevitably turning from one thing which is real and authentic to something else which is much less so. But an illustration may help to clarify why this *must* be the case. Let us suppose that you cross the Atlantic Ocean from east to west on a liner. Inevitably, you are overwhelmed by its immensity, by its sheer size, by the sense of being totally insignificant compared with its vastness. Your experience of the ocean makes a deep impression upon you, and although you find it difficult to express in words, you could make a reasonable attempt at describing it to your friends. You then pick up a map of the western hemisphere and find the Atlantic Ocean reduced to nothing more than some printed lines on a piece of paper. You may be fortunate enough to find the ocean coloured blue and the land masses of America and Europe yellow – but all that you have in your hands is a piece of paper. How on earth does your experience of the Atlantic Ocean relate to it?

First, nobody is going to suggest that the map is a substitute for the real thing. It is an attempt to indicate how various things are related – for example, where Europe and America are situated in relation to each other. It is not even an attempt to scale down the ocean so that you can get the same sort of experience you once had, only on a smaller scale. It is meant to convey certain limited (but important) information, rather than reproduce an authentic experience.

Secondly, the map is based upon the personal experience of countless others, as they also crossed the Atlantic. Whereas your experience is undoubtedly real and important to you, it represents a single, isolated and very personal impression of a much greater reality. Taken on its own, your experience of the Atlantic Ocean is unreliable, perhaps providing your friends with as much information about you as about the ocean itself. The function of the map is to combine as many impressions of a greater reality as possible, in order that a more reliable picture may be built up. The other experiences upon which the map is based are just as vivid and real as yours – but the map eliminates the *personal* element of experience of the Atlantic Ocean in order to provide a more generally reliable guide to the same reality.

The parallels between doctrines and maps will be obvious. First, a doctrine about Jesus was never meant to be a substitute for experience of him – it is simply an attempt to state something limited (but important) about him; to relate him to God and to man, as the map relates the Atlantic Ocean to Europe and America. Thus the rather unexciting formula of the creed, which speaks of Jesus as 'true God and true man', is really just placing Jesus on the map of human experience. Just as the Atlantic Ocean comes between Europe and America, so Jesus at the very least mediates between God and man. Just as the map told the traveller that the Atlantic would lead him from Europe to America, from the Old World to the New, so the doctrine of the 'two natures' of Christ tells us that man encounters God through him.

Refugees fleeing to the United States from persecution or a hopeless economic situation in Europe in the first decades of the twentieth century knew that their hope of a new life lay in crossing the Atlantic Ocean. The deep sense of relief and joy when the New York skyline came into view is well known to us through contemporary films. And so it is with those who are seeking for God, for meaning and hope, in a seemingly dark, meaningless and hopeless world. Through Christ they encounter the living God – the source of their new life, their hope and their joy. Nobody is for one moment suggesting that this is everything that could be said about Jesus, or that it adequately describes the deep personal significance which he holds for each and every believer – but it does help us to begin to locate that significance, to be more precise about it than would otherwise be possible.

Secondly, we all experience Jesus in a different way – he is seen through many eyes, heard through many ears, and loved by many hearts. Inevitably, our attempts to describe this experience are going to be highly impressionistic, probably conveying more information about ourselves than about Jesus. Our backgrounds, our hopes and fears, our understanding of the world – all these things colour our impressions of Jesus. But when countless such experiences are taken into account, the personal element may be eliminated to give a more reliable account of the significance of Jesus, reflecting the consensus of the church down the ages, rather than the impressions of a few individuals.

Doctrines are essentially the distillation of the Christian experience of God, in which countless personal experiences are compared and reduced to their common features. Thus the formula 'true God and true man' is at the very least an attempt to express the conviction that we only know both God and man through Jesus.

Christianity represents a judicious compromise between two extreme views. Although each of these views is correct and important, each is inadequate on its own. On the one hand is the extreme represented by a purely emotional faith which experiences God and trusts implicitly in him but is unable to express itself coherently. Faith unquestionably has a *content* as well as an *object* – in other words, we don't just believe *in* God, we believe certain quite definite things about him. It is the task of every generation in the history of the Christian church to develop an articulate and authoritative account of its faith. The believer is also a thinker, and can never permit his faith to remain or become a shallow uninformed emotionalism. Emotion is an important element of the Christian faith – and those who despise it have no right to do so – but on its own, it is inadequate, incapable of doing justice to the essence of Christian faith.

On the other hand, Christianity is most emphatically not just a list of intellectual propositions to which the believer's assent is demanded. It is grounded in experience. It is worth remembering that Christian belief in the divinity of Christ did not arise as an intellectual theory, but through the impact of experience. The early Christians were thus faced with the intellectual task of thinking through the implications of their experience of Christ as God, and expressing it in as clear and persuasive a manner as possible. The full-blooded nature of Christian faith can never, as we emphasized above, be adequately expressed as propositions, any more than the Atlantic Ocean could be reduced to some marks upon a piece of paper. Furthermore, it is possible for Christianity to degenerate into concern for an intellectual system, rather than for a *person* who enters into our experience and transforms it. The intellectual side of Christian faith is important – but once more, taken on its own, it is inadequate. A judicious compromise, therefore, is necessary in order to preserve both what we might call the subjective and objective aspects of faith. In other words, Christian faith is grounded in experience, but its content may still be summarized in propositions such as 'Jesus is Lord', 'Jesus is the Son of God' or 'Jesus is true God and true man'. There is no inconsistency involved – both the proposition and the experience relate to the same greater reality which lies behind them both. Faith involves both head and heart!

It is interesting to reflect on the reason why the church started laying down doctrines in the first place. It cannot be emphasized too strongly that doctrines are not a set of arbitrary regulations invented by some committee in an orgy of dialectical wrestling. Far from it – doctrines were hammered out at moments when the very heart of the Christian faith seemed to be under threat through simplification, distortion or misunderstanding.

Christian doctrines and dogmas became inevitable when disagreement arose within the church about what the Christian experience of God and Christ actually meant. There was every danger that an understanding of God or Christ would arise which made some sort of sense, but could not do justice to the richness of the Christian experience of God. It is much simpler to believe that Jesus was just a splendid example of humanity, with insights and abilities denied to most of us, than to believe that he is (in some sense of the word) God. The difficulty was that this simply didn't seem to tie in with the way in which Christians experienced Christ, which pointed to a rather different way of looking at him. Some words of T.S. Eliot are worth remembering here: 'We had the experience, but missed the meaning, but approach to the meaning restored the experience.'

Doctrine cannot be isolated from Christian worship and prayer – and the simple fact was that this simpler, neater, more attractive approach to Jesus didn't tie in with the fact that Christians worshipped and adored him, prayed to him, and experienced him in a personal manner. Only by ensuring that doctrine ties in with experience can sense be made of the Christian faith – and once rival theories of Jesus' identity and significance began to appear (such as Arianism), which were so obviously deficient in this respect, the church *had* to make some sort of response. And so doctrines were hammered out and then expressed in creeds. They were never meant to be a substitute for Christian experience – just a sort of 'hedge', marking out an area of thought about God and Christ which seemed to be faithful to Christian experience.

Some words of Thomas Carlyle are worth noting here: 'If the Arians had won, Christianity would have dwindled to a legend.' Experience and meaning would have drifted apart to the point where eventually both were lost. It is simply not true that doctrine is a hopeless irrelevance to the life and work of the Christian church; it is one of the few safeguards by which its identity and relevance have been, and still are, preserved in the face of a disbelieving world.

There is still, of course, widespread reluctance in some quarters to allow Jesus Christ any claim to be God in any meaningful sense of the word. The popular idea of Christianity is still that Jesus Christ was a great moral teacher and that mankind would profit greatly if they took his advice seriously. Of course, there have been other outstanding teachers before Jesus and after him – men like Plato, Aristotle, Confucius and so on – who have also had some words of wisdom for mankind. The popular idea of Christianity gives Jesus place of honour among such men, but whatever difference there may be between them is one of degree, rather than kind. They are all basically human beings, enlightened to various degrees, who have contributed to (or at least *tried* to contribute to) the moral education of man.

The first difficulty associated with this view is that it is only too painfully obvious that man has tended never to pay much attention to his teachers. Man has had plenty of good moral advice over the last three or four thousand years, and that given by Jesus is unlikely to make much diference if it isn't followed. Indeed, we might go further and suggest that there appears to be something about human nature which makes it impossible to take good advice. Something more than education is required if man's situation is to be altered for the better.

The second difficulty, however, is even more serious. Christians simply don't view Jesus in this way. They just don't treat Jesus as a super-rabbi. They talk about Jesus being the 'Bread of Life', or the 'Lamb of God, who takes away the sin of the world'. They will undoubtedly make reference to – and value – Jesus' moral teaching, but their main interest concerns the significance of his death and resurrection. Just as with St Paul, interest in the crucified and risen Christ has almost completely overshadowed his teaching ministry. Good teachers, after all, are not that difficult to find. People who are crucified, only to be raised from the dead, are somewhat thinner on the ground, and command attention for that very reason.

Christians have never looked back to Palestine to revere the memory of a dead teacher (in other words, a rabbi), but have looked up (if anywhere) to worship a living Lord. However difficult the terms may be, the fact is that Christians have tended to designate the crucified and risen Jesus as 'Lord', 'Son of God' or 'Saviour', and have gathered together on the day of the week marking his resurrection to worship him as their Saviour and Lord, rather than just learn from him as their Teacher.

We can learn much from the history of the Christian church in the first few centuries of its existence. First, it is clear that Christians had no hesitation in worshipping Christ as God. This practice was noted by the younger Pliny in his famous letter of A.D. 112 to the Emperor Trajan, in which he reports that Christians sang hymns to their Lord 'as God' (*quasi deo*). The views of one early maverick theologian, to the effect that Christ was merely a rather special man, was answered with an appeal to the universal Christian practice of singing 'psalms and songs written from the beginning by faithful brethren, which celebrate the Word of God, that is Christ, and speak of him as God'. The heretic bishop Paul of Samosata, deposed in A.D. 268, attempted to stop his congregations worshipping Christ, recognizing that this well-established practice – which, of course, continues to the present day – posed an irrefutable challenge to his own view that Christ was not divine (in any meaningful sense of the word).

The Arian controversy of the early fourth century serves to highlight these points. Arius, while giving Christ precedence over all of God's creatures, insisted that he was still nothing more than a creature, rather than God. Although Jesus was to be treated as the first among men, he was still a man, and nothing more than a man. Two major lines of argument were advanced against him by his orthodox opponent Athanasius. First, he repeated the point we have just noted. Arius, he suggested, was making the entire church guilty of worshipping a creature, rather than God. Only God could be worshipped, argued Athanasius, and as Christians had worshipped Christ from the beginning of the Christian era, this meant that Christ had to be regarded as divine. We can see here an argument from Christ's *function* (as an object of worship) to his *identity* (as God who alone may be worshipped).

Secondly, Athanasius argued that created beings cannot be saved by another created being. Only God can save – and as Christ saves man (which Arius did not, incidentally, dispute), he must be treated as God. Once more, we can see a direct argument from Christ's function (as Saviour) to his identity (as God).

The early Christians, then, worshipped Christ as a fully divine saviour, regarding this as the obvious interpretation of the New Testament material. This basic understanding of the identity and function of Jesus Christ has remained characteristic of Christianity since then, despite a number of challenges to this understanding from within, as well as from outside, the Christian church. One such challenge is particularly interesting, and is worth considering in some detail. This is the so-called 'Quest for the Historical Jesus' which culminated in the last century.

The period of rationalism in Europe, usually regarded as having begun in the eighteenth century, showed little taste for ideas such as Jesus being a divine saviour. If Jesus was anything, according to the rationalists, he was a good moral teacher. It was argued that ideas such as Jesus being a divine saviour were actually due to early Christians misunderstanding or misrepresenting the New Testament, and that it was possible to rediscover the *real* Jesus by approaching the New Testament in a different way. This suggestion should, perhaps, have been viewed with considerably more scepticism than it actually encountered. After all, every week undergraduate theologians, and every year or so some plodding American associate professor of religious studies, 'discover' for the very first time exactly what Paul's theology, or the death of Jesus, was *really* about, and find themselves astonished at the lack of excitement and interest their discovery evokes. But the fact remains that some nineteenth-century New Testament scholars felt that it was possible to recover the 'real' Jesus from the Jesus of Christianity.

According to these scholars, the early church got Jesus completely wrong. He wasn't God incarnate or a divine saviour, but a moral teacher whose views on most things happened – remarkably – to coincide with those of his rediscoverers. Jesus was the teacher of the Fatherhood of God and the Brotherhood of Man – an essentially simple and modern message, for which the first eighteen centuries of the Christian church were totally unprepared and were obliged to leave to modern scholars to take up. The pearl of great price, having only just been dug up, was immediately reburied in the hope that some wise and benevolent professor of theology might rediscover it centuries later. It was nothing less than a matter of divine providence that men, living nineteen hundred years after his death, and sharing nothing of his culture, his background, his language and his presuppositions, should be able to get Jesus right – when his contemporaries, who shared his culture, background, language and presuppositions should have got him so terribly wrong. And the fact that the rediscovered Jesus was practically the mirror image of his rediscoverers was purely fortuitous! It just so happened that Jesus actually taught all the right things by the standards of the nineteenth century – the principles which ensure the healthy progress of civilization, morality and so on.

The possibility that these idealist theologians of the nineteenth century might just have projected their own moral ideas and aspirations onto a distant historical figure, about whom they knew practically nothing, in order to discredit a different understanding of the identity and significance of Jesus, for which they cared even less, never seems to have entered their heads.

Since then, of course, we have been presented with lots of rediscovered Jesuses. He was a freedom fighter, an itinerant Kantian, a hypnotist, a mushroom-eater and a confused prophet, to name but a few. In fact, it is difficult to avoid the impression that there are a lot of people arguing that, whoever Jesus was, he *definitely wasn't* the divine saviour of sinful man that Christians have always thought he was. Because Jesus couldn't be God incarnate, they argued, he must have been something else. Curiously, their views on who Jesus really was turned out to be even more unbelievable, although it took some time for this point to be fully appreciated.

In the following chapter we shall look at the nature of the New Testament sources which oblige us to dismiss such 'rediscovered Jesuses' as interesting, but quite unjustifiable, products of overactive human imaginations.

3

The Sources of Our Knowledge about Jesus

We are almost totally dependent upon the New Testament, and particularly the first three gospels, for our knowledge about Jesus. Although there are early documents other than the New Testament writings which make reference to Jesus, or the beliefs of Christians about him, these are of little interest to any except specialist historians. But just what sort of documents are the gospels?

In the last chapter we met the 'Quest for the Historical Jesus' movement which attempted to sift through Christian beliefs about Jesus to find the 'real' Jesus who lay behind them. Christianity had got Jesus wrong – it was time to get him right! One of the assumptions made by the movement was that the gospels, particularly the Synoptic Gospels (that is, Matthew, Mark and Luke) could be treated as historical sources. In other words, the gospels were treated as if they were completely impartial documents which merely recorded facts (rather than opinions) about Jesus. It was then up to the individual reader of the gospels to make sense of these facts as best he could.

In practice, of course, most of those engaged in the 'Quest for the Historical Jesus' found themselves turning a blind eye to those facts recorded in the gospels which they found difficult to cope with. Their desire to discover a simple moral teacher in Jesus led them to ignore, or attempt to explain away, certain facts recorded by the gospels which didn't fit their preconceived pattern. For example, the gospel accounts of Jesus' resurrection clearly imply that Jesus was infinitely more than a wandering Jewish moralist – and so these were ignored or rationalized as misunderstandings.

Similarly, the gospel accounts of Jesus' preoccupation with his forthcoming death at the hands of the leaders of his own people were something of an embarrassment, and were passed over in much the same way. The real significance of Jesus, according to this movement, was his teaching, particularly as expressed in the Sermon on the Mount and the parables, all of which could be expressed morally.

But why were the gospels written in the first place? And how can we explain the way in which the material is arranged within the gospels? And, perhaps even more important, what factors determined the material to be included in the gospels?

All too often, the scholars of the nineteenth century seem to have assumed that the gospels were written for their convenience; a collection of sayings of Jesus which they could interpret as they pleased. If something didn't appeal to the reinterpreters of Jesus, they felt able to pass over it or explain it away. Since the final decade of the nineteenth century, however, it has become clear that the gospels simply cannot be treated in this superficial way. The first three gospels are, indeed, reliable sources of knowledge concerning Jesus. That point has been confirmed, rather than called into question, by responsible New Testament scholarship. But what has become increasingly clear is that this knowledge takes a particular form which cannot be ignored when it comes to interpreting it. So let us look at the broad features of the gospel accounts of Jesus in order to appreciate this point.

The gospels weren't written by Jesus himself, nor do they date from his lifetime. It is generally thought that Jesus was crucified about the year A.D. 30, and that the earliest gospel (probably Mark) dates from about A.D. 65. In other words, there is probably a gap of about thirty years between the events taking place and their being recorded in the form of a gospel. What happened in between?

It is difficult for the twentieth-century reader to understand why so long a gap existed between the events and their recording. We are used to information being recorded in the *written* form, and easily forget that the primitive world communicated by means of the *spoken* word. The great Homeric epics are good examples of the way in which stories were passed on with remarkable faithfulness from one generation to another.

If there is one ability which modern man has probably lost, it is the ability to *remember* a story or narrative as it is told, and then to pass it on to others afterwards. As one study after another of primitive culture confirms, the passing down of stories from one generation to another was characteristic of the pre-modern era – including the time of the New Testament itself. Indeed, there are excellent grounds for arguing that early educational systems were based upon learning by rote. The fact that we find it difficult to commit even a short story or narrative to memory naturally tends to prejudice us against believing that anyone else could do it – and yet it is evident that it was done, and was done remarkably well. Indeed, this ability has not been completely lost. I can remember very clearly how a friend described his astonishment when an elderly Jew whom he knew was able to recite the entire Old Testament in Hebrew from memory, while being checked against the printed text!

The period between the death of Jesus and the writing of the first gospel is usually referred to as the 'period of oral tradition', meaning the period in which acounts of Jesus' birth, life and death, as well as his teaching, were passed down with remarkable faithfulness from one generation to another.

In this period, it seems that certain sayings of Jesus and certain aspects of his life (especially his death and resurrection) were singled out as being of particular importance, and were passed down from the first Christians to those who followed them. Others were not passed down, and have been lost for ever. The early Christians seem to have identified what was essential, and what was not so important, among Jesus' words, deeds and fate, and passed down only the former to us.

An excellent example of this process of transmission may be found in Paul's first letter to the Christians at Corinth, almost certainly dating from the period of oral transmission:

> For I received from the Lord what I also delivered to you, that the Lord Jesus on the night when he was betrayed took bread, and when he had given thanks, he broke it, and said, ' ... Do this in remembrance of me.' In the same way also the cup, after supper, saying, 'This cup is the new covenant in my blood. Do this, as often as you drink it, in remembrance of me' (1 Corinthians 11:23–25).

It is clear that Paul is passing something on to the Corinthian Christians which had been passed on to him, presumably by word of mouth. It is interesting to compare these verses with their equivalents in the gospels (Matthew 26:26–28; Mark 14:22–24; Luke 22:17–19).

The 'period of oral tradition' may thus be regarded as a period of 'sifting', in which the first Christians assessed what was necessary to pass down to those who followed them. Thus Jesus' sayings may have become detached from their original context, and perhaps on occasion even been given a new one, simply through the use to which the first Christians put them – proclaiming the gospel to those outside the early community of faith, and deepening and informing the faith of those inside it. There is every reason to suppose that those early Christians preserved and transmitted faithfully the *substance* and the *meaning* of Jesus' teaching and actions, even if it is conceivable that some slight inaccuracies in the precise wording of Jesus' sayings, or the chronology of his actions, may have arisen. The early Christians weren't parrots – they were preachers.

Although the gospel writers did indeed pass on to their readers authentic traditions concerning Jesus, those traditions were selected on the basis of the needs of the early Christian church, as it sought to spread the gospel. Perhaps John's gospel states this point most clearly:

> Now Jesus did many other signs in the presence of the disciples, which are not written in this book, but these [i.e., the ones that *are* included] are written that you may believe that Jesus is the Christ, the Son of God, and that believing you may have life in his name (John 20:30–31).

This passage states two things explicitly. First, the principle of *selectivity*. The gospel writers have been selective in their material (note also John 21:25), following the oral tradition passed down to them. Much information about Jesus has been lost for ever, simply because the early Christians did not feel that it was of any relevance to their purposes of evangelization and teaching.

Secondly, the gospels were written with a purpose in mind – that of conversion, of generating faith in their readers. To develop this point, we must return to the distinction between *event* and *interpretation* discussed in chapter one.

As we noted in that chapter, Christianity is not primarily concerned with the events associated with Jesus Christ, but with the interpretation of the significance of those events. The gospel writers were not concerned primarily with recording the events of the life and death of Jesus, but with indicating their significance. We could say that they mingle history and interpretation, in that they indicate the significance of events, rather than merely recording them. Thus in the passage just quoted from John's gospel, the evangelist is clearly drawing a distinction between 'signs' (events) and 'believing that Jesus is the Christ, the Son of God' (interpretation). Similarly, we find Paul appealing to an oral

tradition which combines the report of events (Jesus' death
and resurrection) with the interpretation of these events
(forgiveness of sins) in 1 Corinthians 15:3–5 (a passage discussed in chapter one).

Some immortal words from Edmund Clerihew Bentley's
Biography for Beginners are worth noting here:

> The art of Biography
> Is different from Geography.
> Geography is about maps,
> But Biography is about chaps.

It is, of course, always useful to be reminded of this important point. We may be able to distinguish between geography
and biography without too much difficulty, but distinguish-
ing between biography and theology in the gospels is much
more difficult. The gospel writers were not biographers, or
even historians, by our standards, nor were they even remotely interested in giving an exhaustive or totally precise
account of everything that Jesus said and did. It did not
matter to them at precisely what point in his ministry Jesus
told a particular parable, for example – the important thing
was that he *did* tell it, and that it was realized to be relevant
to the preaching of the early church.

It is obvious that the gospels of Matthew, Mark and Luke
draw upon common material, although at times we encounter material which is peculiar to one, or two, gospels. The
same material is sometimes presented in one setting in Mark,
another in Matthew, and perhaps even a third in Luke.
Sometimes the same story is told from different perspectives
in different gospels. Sometimes a story is told at greater
length in one gospel than in another.

It is evident that there is an historical core to the gospels,
underlying the variations encountered in the gospel accounts.
New Testament scholarship has merely clarified the nature
of this historical core rather than called it into question. But
it is also obvious that the gospel writers were simply not

interested in reproducing precise historical accounts of everything which Jesus said and did. For them, 'historical' simply meant 'based on historical fact', not 'a strictly exact chronological account of absolutely everything which Jesus said and did'. There can be no doubt whatsoever that the gospel accounts of Jesus contain a solid base of historical information linked with an interpretation of that information – in other words, biography and theology mixed up to such an extent that they can't be separated any more. The early Christians were convinced that Jesus was the Messiah, the Son of God and their Saviour, and naturally felt that these conclusions should be passed on to their readers, along with any biographical details which helped cast light on them. It is for this reason that fact and interpretation are so thoroughly intermingled in the gospels. The first Christians had no doubt that their theological interpretation of Jesus was right, and that it was therefore an important fact which should be included in their 'biographies'.

With this point in mind, let us return to the ill-fated 'Quest for the Historical Jesus'. The basic assumption which lay behind this movement was that the gospels were essentially factual accounts of the history of Jesus, which could be interpreted by the reader. Or, to put it another way, the gospels were treated as raw data which required interpretation. We now know that this is quite unacceptable. The gospels are not purely factual, but intermingle history and theology, event and interpretation. They are not 'raw data' requiring interpretation, but are interpretations of 'raw data'.

Furthermore, the process of selection which is so important a feature of the 'period of oral transmission' means that much information concerning him (which the early Christians thought insignificant for their purposes) is for ever lost. As a result, the reader of the gospels does not have access to the material which he would need if he was to attempt a realistic 'reinterpretation' of Jesus. The gospels are written from the standpoint of faith in the crucified and risen Jesus, and reflect the faith of the early Christians to such an extent that it is actually impossible to distinguish between 'event' and 'interpretation' at points. The gospels are written in the light of the fundamental conviction that Jesus is 'the Christ, the Son of the living God' (Matthew 16:16), and their content cannot actually be isolated from this conviction.

This point presents no difficulties whatsoever for the Christian reader of the gospel, who shares the faith of the gospel writers concerning the identity and significance of Jesus Christ. It does, however, raise certain fundamental difficulties for those who do not share this faith. Basically, the gospels are out to win their readers over to their point of view about the identity and significance of Jesus by setting the reader alongside the disciples as they come to faith in order that he may share the same experience. But the reader who is convinced that the first Christians were wrong in their understanding of the identity and significance of Jesus – and hence that the gospels are wrong at certain crucial points – is faced with three possible options.

First, he may argue that the gospels allow him to develop a different interpretation of the identity and significance of Jesus which he finds more plausible. This is essentially the approach of the 'Quest for the Historical Jesus' movement. This approach is initially attractive, but on further reflection is obviously impossible. To reinterpret Jesus requires access to information which is no longer available to us – the *complete* history of Jesus Christ, absolutely everything which he said and did, as well as a total familiarity with the first-century Palestinian culture in which his ministry took place. This history is for ever lost to us. All that we possess of it is what we find in the gospels – and it will be obvious that the gospel writers have been selective in regard to what they included!

Furthermore, history and theology, event and interpretation, are intermingled to such an extent that they cannot be separated with the accuracy and precision which such a re-interpretation would require. The 'reinterpretation' of Jesus *on the basis of the New Testament accounts* is thus a blind alley which leads nowhere.

It is, of course, possible to base a 'reinterpretation' of Jesus on something other than the gospels, such as preconceived ideas about God or man, but this is of little relevance to the Christian understanding of the identity and significance of Christ, particularly as Christians have generally based their understandings of God and man upon Jesus, rather than the other way round. For example, he may say that as God is absolutely beyond this world, he could not have become incarnate. (Anyway, how does he know this? How can he be *sure* that this is what God is really like? Has he access to some source of knowledge denied to everyone else, which allows him to make such certain statements about God?)

The Christian, however, argues the other way round – *because* God *did* become incarnate, we must learn to reject any concept of God which means that he must be thought of as being totally beyond this world, and uninvolved in it. Preconceived ideas about God must be abandoned and replaced with the God whom we see, know and meet in Jesus Christ.

The argument really concerns how we know about God in the first place. The Christian argues that the person of Jesus is the most reliable source of knowledge about God to be had, whereas others may argue you can learn about him from the night sky, or sunsets, or nice paintings. We shall return to this argument in chapter seven.

Secondly, he may reject the gospels completely, and have nothing to do with them. This is an intellectually honest approach, but one which is not likely to commend itself to Christological sceptics!

Thirdly, he may approach the gospels in the spirit in which they were written, either sharing the faith of the gospel writers, or allowing himself to be carried along with them. Once more, this approach has the virtue of intellectual honesty. The reader may wish to attempt to restate the convictions of the gospel writers in terms more comprehensible to the modern reader, but he is still operating within the framework of faith established by the gospels.

The new understanding of the nature of the gospels which has developed over the last century thus cannot be said to have eroded confidence in the reliability of the New Testament portrayal of Christ, despite the swashbuckling claims of overenthusiastic critics of Christianity. New Testament scholarship has established that the gospels are a remarkable, probably a unique, form of writing, and has helped us to understand the purposes, intentions and priorities of their writers with greater confidence. This new approach does, however, devastate a number of rival approaches to the identity and significance of Jesus.

The father of the modern critical approach to the New Testament was the great Marburg New Testament scholar and theologian, Rudolf Bultmann, who emphasized two points. First, the critical approach to the New Testament cut the ground from under liberal Christologies (such as Jesus as just a 'teacher' or 'moral example'). Secondly, there was an urgent need to restate the *content* of the New Testament portrayal of Christ in terms that modern man could make sense of. We are particularly concerned with the first of these points here, and will return to the second in a later chapter.

For Bultmann, the New Testament witnessed to an understanding of Jesus as an act of God, totally distinct from anything else. This understanding of the identity and significance of Jesus is deeply embedded in the New Testament, particularly the gospels, to the extent that it was quite impossible to find any other picture of Jesus portrayed in its pages. Bultmann thus singled out three understandings of the identity and significance of Jesus which could no longer be taken seriously. First, there was the view that Jesus was just a good religious teacher, like Moses. Secondly, there was the view that Jesus was a religious hero, who died to make some sort of religious point. Thirdly, there was the view that Jesus' significance lay in his religious personality or his consciousness of the presence of God.

The foundations of all these were, according to Bultmann, shattered beyond repair by the rise of a critical study of the New Testament. According to Bultmann, the only understanding of the identity and significance of Jesus which could stand up in the light of New Testament scholarship was that of a unique divine act in human history. How Bultmann went on to explain this divine act does not concern us here, and is actually not relevant to our discussion. What *is* important is the realization that if *any* understanding of the identity and significance of Jesus has been irredeemably discredited by modern New Testament scholarship, it is *not* what we might call the 'traditional' picture of Christ as being God and man, but the views of the 'rediscoverers of the historical Jesus' and their modern-day followers.

Of course, there are still those who will wish to suggest that Jesus was a religious genius, or hero, or just a lunatic – indeed, there will almost certainly always be views like this in circulation. But what needs to be emphasized is that they cannot be supported by responsible use of the New Testament documents, and particularly the gospels, as sources. And as we are almost totally dependent upon precisely these sources for our knowledge of Jesus, this virtually amounts to the elimination of such totally inadequate portrayals of the identity and significance of Jesus Christ. It is ironical, to say the least, that some critics of traditional Christianity appeal to Bultmann in support of their views about Jesus being a moral example, or a religious teacher – apparently quite unaware that it was against exactly these views that Bultmann directed his devastating criticisms!

Let us now return to the Synoptic Gospels (Matthew, Mark and Luke), and look more closely at the way they

portray Christ. It is clear that the gospels are not biographies, although they do indeed contain a hard core of
historical information about Jesus. Nor are they religious
textbooks spelling out the basics of Christian ethics, although they do indeed contain much teaching concerning
morality. Perhaps the most helpful way of thinking of them is
to draw a parallel with a somewhat different type of modern
literary form – the detective novel.

The essence of every good detective novel lies in engaging
the reader in the detective's search for the murderer. In
effect, the reader is set alongside the fictional detective as he
discovers clues, and gradually builds up a picture of what
must have happened in order to uncover the identity of the
murderer in an exciting climax. It is only at this point that the
reader finds out whether he has noticed all the clues and
worked out their significance. Of course, there is always
something of a temptation for the author of such novels to
introduce so many 'red herrings' that it is difficult to distinguish them from real clues. And certain novelists – Agatha
Christie comes to mind immediately as an example – even
conceal clues from the reader in order to hold his interest to
the final chapter.

In several respects, the gospels parallel this type of writing. The reader of the gospels is set alongside the disciples as
they listen to Jesus preach, as they watch him in action, and
as they finally see him die and raised again. But whereas
detective novels are basically 'Whodunits', the gospels are
'Whowasits'. In other words, we are concerned with establishing the identity and significance of their central figure,
rather than with picking out a murderer from a number of
possible suspects. The gospel writers allow us to see and hear
what the disciples heard, and force us to ask much the same
questions which they themselves must have asked before us.
Who is this man? And just as the writers of detective novels
single out, or draw our attention to, significant things (in
other words, clues) which we might otherwise have over-

looked, so the gospel writers do the same. Before we illustrate this with some examples, an important point needs to be made.

It is all too easy to overlook clues, for a number of reasons. For example, something may take place which appears to be insignificant at the time, and yet assumes a much greater significance later, as its full meaning becomes obvious. Thus in Arthur Conan Doyle's story *Silver Blaze*, the full significance of the fact that the dog did *not* bark during the night only becomes evident at a late stage. The *fact* is observed, but its *significance* only becomes apparent later. The author is thus obliged to single out this one apparently insignificant fact (and ignore other apparently equally insignificant facts) because it was later realized to be relevant. He has to be selective, 'filtering' out facts which he knows (on account of later developments) to be important, and ignoring others which he knows are not so important (even though this may not have been obvious at the time at which they took place).

There is every reason to suppose that something similar has happened in the case of the gospels. The first Christians appear to have realized the full significance of some of the things which Jesus said or did after his resurrection, when they suddenly saw things in a completely new light. An apparently insignificant fact thus assumed a new meaning, simply because its full significance was realized – perhaps late in the day, but better late than never. Thus in John's gospel we find an explicit reference to this process. Jesus makes a remark which appears to refer to the temple at Jerusalem, whereas after the resurrection his disciples realized that it referred to Jesus himself (John 2:18–22).

It is clear that some clues concerning the identity and significance were impossible to overlook – the resurrection itself being the most obvious example. Others, however, appear to have been more subtle – they were only recognized for what they really were after the resurrection when the penny finally dropped for the disciples. This point serves to remind us that the gospel accounts are meant to be read in the light of faith in the resurrection, which the early Christians evidently took as fundamental to their beliefs about Jesus. And sometimes the fact that something *didn't* happen is important – just as it was important to Sherlock Holmes that the dog didn't bark in the night when the racehorse Silver Blaze was stolen, when it might have been expected to. Thus Mark notes that Jesus was silent before his accusers (Mark 14:61), when he might have been expected to defend himself. The significance of this silence can be seen in the light of the silence of the Suffering Servant (Isaiah 53:7) before his accusers. Mark appears to want us to pick up this clue, and draws us on to note other parallels between Jesus and this mysterious Old Testament figure (which we will note in a moment). Let us now return to the gospel narratives.

It is evident that Matthew initially wants us to draw the conclusion that Jesus was the Messiah, the long-expected descendant of King David who was expected to usher in a new era in the history of Israel. The first part of his gospel is therefore littered with clues pointing to this conclusion. Thus the gospel opens with a list of Jesus' forefathers (Matthew 1:1–17) which establishes that Jesus was legally the son of David – as the Messiah ought to have been. We are then given an account of the birth of Jesus in which Matthew makes sure that we don't overlook the remark-able parallels between the circumstances of that birth and the prophecies of the Old Testament. Thus Matthew draws our attention to this point no less than five times (Matthew 1:22–23; 2:5–7; 2:16; 2:17–18; 2:23) in his first two chapters.

Mark's gospel opens by establishing the credentials of John the Baptist. John is the long-expected messenger who prepares the way for the coming of the Lord (Mark 1:2–3). Having established this point, Mark records John's statement that someone even more significant will come after him (Mark 1:7–8). And who is it Mark immediately introduces to us? 'In those days Jesus came from Nazareth of Galilee and was baptized by John in the Jordan' (Mark 1:9). The conclusion Mark wishes us to draw is obvious.

Although some of the clues concerning the identity and significance of Jesus are pointed out with some force, others are left to the reader to pick up for himself. For example, Jesus regularly addresses God as 'Father' in his prayers – a very presumptuous practice by the standards of that time. At one point, Mark even gives us the Aramaic original of the word for 'Father' – *Abba*, a remarkably familiar term impossible to translate into English ('Papa', 'Dad' and 'Daddy' often being suggested as the nearest equivalents). The gospel writers do not bring out the full significance of this practice which clearly points to Jesus understanding himself to have a remarkably intimate relationship to God.

Equally, the remarkable parallels between the Righteous Sufferer of Psalm 22 and the accounts of Christ's passion are not made explicit, but are left unsaid. Jesus' words 'My God, my God, why hast thou forsaken me?' (Matthew 27:46) – the only point, incidentally, at which Jesus does not address God as 'Father' – draw our attention to this mysterious Psalm, and particularly to certain of its descriptions of the mode of death of the Righteous Sufferer. The Righteous Sufferer is mocked by those who watch him die (Psalm 22:6–8) – as is Jesus (Matthew 27:39–44). The Righteous Sufferer has his hands and feet pierced (Psalm 22:16) – as would most victims of crucifixion, including Jesus. The Righteous Sufferer sees his tormentors casting lots for his clothes (Psalm 22:18) – as does Jesus (Matthew 27:35). Another remarkable parallel exists between the crucifixion and the account of the Suffering Servant of Isaiah 53, which only Luke notes explicitly (Luke 22:37). This famous Old Testament prophecy speaks of a Suffering Servant of God, who was 'wounded for our transgressions, [and] bruised for our iniquities (Isaiah 53:5).

Perhaps the most significant part of this prophecy relates to the fact that the Servant is 'numbered with the transgressors' (Isaiah 53:12), which is clearly understood by the gospel writers to be paralleled in two manners. First, Christ died by crucifixion, which, as we emphasized in chapter one, was a mode of death reserved for criminals. In other words, Christ was identified with sinners by the manner of his death. Secondly, Christ was not crucified alone, but along with two criminals (Matthew 27:38). In both ways, Christ's death paralleled that of an important Old Testament figure.

Other parallels with this account may be seen in the gospels, although they are not pointed out by the gospel writers. Thus Luke notes that Jesus prayed for his executioners (Luke 23:34), paralleling the actions of the Suffering Servant (Isaiah 53:12). In fact, it seems that the first Christians could not help but notice the obvious parallels between the life and death of Jesus and certain significant prophecies of the Old Testament, and take a certain degree of delight in pointing them out to their readers, or allowing them to discover them for themselves.

As we have seen, the evangelists were theologians, rather than biographers, painting a portrait which attempted to bring out the full richness of their impressions of Jesus Christ. When looking at a painting, such as a landscape, we can of course concentrate our attention upon one part of it, examining the small detail underlying the artist's work. The great portrayal of a Flemish landscape may, on closer examination, disclose astonishing attention to detail in individual blades of grass. But it is the overall impression which the picture conveys that is of crucial importance. After marvelling at the landscape, our attention may wander to consider the intricacy of the artwork on the blades of grass, as one component of that landscape, of that greater whole of which it is a part. But it is the overall impression and impact which really counts.

Jesus came to those who first knew him as a living man, a totality rather than a sum of small parts. Later, as the first Christians reflected on the astonishing personality of Jesus, they were able to discriminate between the various elements which contributed to the impression he made upon them. But this is something which happened later, after the passage of time allowed such an analysis to take place. The immediate impression which Jesus made upon those whom he encountered is what underlies this analysis. What was it about Jesus that caused those fishermen to drop their nets, leave everything and follow him into the unknown? What was it that caused people to marvel at his teaching?

With remarkable skill, the evangelists paint for us a portrait of Christ as the King of Israel, the Servant of the Lord, the Friend of Sinners and the Word Incarnate. This building up of a portrait of Jesus Christ as Saviour and Lord was not done in some clumsy or haphazard way, like a child cutting up bits of paper and pasting them into a scrapbook, but in a genuinely artistic process through which material is brought together in the mind of the evangelist as a consistent whole. It is this consistent portrayal of Christ which finds its expression in the gospels. We must realize that behind the wealth of detail which we find in the gospels lies an attempt to express the totality of Jesus Christ. The details are like brush-strokes which build up to form a portrait. A brush-stroke taken on its own is inadequate to disclose the whole vision of the painter. There is every danger that as we study the gospels we will fail to see the wood for the trees, the portrait for the brush-strokes, the landscape for the blades of grass. If you look at a television screen very closely, you will see that the picture is made up of very small coloured dots – but to see the picture you have to stand back, losing sight of this detail, as the dots merge to form a picture.

We must learn to stand back from the small details of Jesus in order to grasp him as a whole. The details merge and

Christ as Saviour and Lord emerges. We will overlook the portrayal of Christ as Saviour and Lord as we concentrate upon the parables or the passion narratives. We must learn to see these as pieces of a jigsaw, as intricate detail in a work of art, all combining to disclose Jesus to us as he once disclosed himself to his disciples.

The gospels portray the gradual dawn of faith in the disciples. Initially, they see in Jesus a great teacher – one who taught with authority, unlike their own teachers (Mark 1:27). Gradually, other insights begin to develop. For example, Jesus performs signs and wonders which arouse enormous popular interest in him throughout the region. Eventually, they have sufficient information at their disposal to come to the conclusion which marks a turning point in the gospel narratives: the confession that Jesus is the Messiah (Matthew 16:16; Mark 8:29; Luke 9:20). Once the disciples have achieved this basic insight, Jesus tells them that he must be rejected by his own people, suffer, be killed and rise again (Matthew 16:21; Mark 8:31; Luke 9:22). The emphasis upon the fact that this *must* happen, and the use of 'be killed', rather than simply 'die', indicates that the early Christians regarded Christ's death as an integral part of his ministry and mission – a fact which is perfectly obvious from the remaining writings of the New Testament, even if the gospels do not choose to emphasize it.

The first Christians did not simply regard Jesus' death as an untimely end to the promising career of a radical rabbi, but as one of the two culminating points of Jesus' mission (the other being his resurrection). Jesus' teaching, important and distinctive though it unquestionably is, assumes its full significance only through the recognition of who Jesus *is*. To put it very crudely: if you have good reason to think that you are dealing with someone who may well be God incarnate, you are likely to take what he says and does a lot more seriously than you would otherwise!

At this point we have sufficient information at our disposal to begin looking seriously at the question of the identity and significance of Jesus. In the second part of this work we shall look at the question of who Jesus is (or 'Christology', to give this aspect of Christian theology its proper name).

PART 2
The Person of Jesus Christ

4

The Resurrection Event

St Paul opens his letter to the Christians at Rome by making a crucially important statement concerning Jesus Christ. According to Paul, Jesus 'was descended from David according to the flesh and designated Son of God ... by his resurrection from the dead' (Romans 1:3–4). This brief statement identifies two grounds on which Jesus should be regarded as the Son of God. First, on the physical level, he was a descendent of David. A similar point is made by Matthew as he opens his gospel (Matthew 1:1). Secondly, Jesus' resurrection established his identity as the Son of God, clinching other arguments to the same effect, such as those we find in the gospels. It is obvious that Paul assumes the resurrection really to have taken place, and that the important thing is to establish what it means. Today, however, the suggestion that Jesus might have risen from the dead is treated with scepticism by many. Before we can begin to ask what the resurrection means, we first have to establish the probability that the resurrection took place at all. So let us begin this chapter by looking at the evidence.

The first point to be made is that the theme of the resurrection occurs throughout the New Testament, and in the preaching of the early church in the period after the completion of the New Testament writings. This obviously doesn't prove that the resurrection took place; what it does prove beyond any reasonable doubt is that the first Christians – indeed, the first *generations* of Christians – regarded the resurrection as an essential, and in some cases perhaps even the central element of the Christian faith. But why? Why should the suggestion that Jesus was actually raised from the dead have become universally accepted among the first Christians?

After two thousand years, Christians have got used to the idea of Jesus being raised from the dead – but the idea is actually very strange. Indeed, by the standards of the first century, it was an extraordinary belief. A much more plausible idea would be that God had exalted Jesus to heaven.

As is well known, there was a widespread belief within Jewish circles in the resurrection of the dead at the time of Jesus. Indeed, Paul was able to exploit the differences between the Pharisees and Sadducees on this point during an awkward moment in his career (see Acts 23:6–8). But this belief concerned the *future* resurrection of the dead, at the end of time itself. The Christian claim was that Jesus had been raised *now*, before the end of time. When Paul refers to Jesus as the 'first-fruits' of the resurrection (1 Corinthians 15:20–23), he means that he was the first of many to rise from the dead – that Jesus had, indeed, been raised before anyone else. This is quite different from Jewish ideas about the resurrection.

So there was something quite distinct and unusual about the Christian claim that Jesus had been raised from the dead, which makes it rather difficult to account for. Why should the first Christians have adopted what was by the standards of their time such a strange belief? The first Christians didn't adopt a widespread Jewish belief, as some have suggested – they altered it dramatically. What the Jews thought could only happen at the end of the world was recognized to have happened in human history, *before* the end of time, and to have been seen and witnessed to by many. This was a startlingly new belief, and its very novelty raises the question of where it came from. Why did the first Christians adopt this belief? The event of the resurrection of Jesus, it would seem, caused them to break with the traditional belief concerning the resurrection. There can be no doubt that the first disciples *did* believe that Jesus had been raised by God. What we must ask is whether they were right in believing this.

Secondly, the tradition concerning the empty tomb is so important an element in each of the four gospels (Matthew 28:1–10; Mark 16:1–8; Luke 24:1–11; John 20:1–10) that it must be considered to have a basis in historical fact. The story is told from different aspects, and includes the divergence on minor points of detail which is so characteristic of eye-witness reports.

Curiously, all four gospels attribute the discovery of the empty tomb to women. At that time the testimony of a woman was virtually worthless. In first-century Palestine this would have been sufficient to discredit the accounts altogether. If the reports of the empty tomb were invented, it is difficult to understand why their inventors should have embellished their accounts of the 'discovery' with something virtually guaranteed to discredit them. Were the first Christians really that stupid? Why not attribute this discovery to *men*, if the story was just invented?

The most obvious explanation is that it was such a widely accepted tradition within the early church that the discoverers of the empty tomb were women that the idea could not be modified, even to make the story of the discovery more plausible.

Furthermore, we know something about the common practice of 'tomb veneration' – returning to the tomb of a prophet as a place of worship. This practice appears to have been widespread at the time of Jesus. Matthew 23:29–30 almost certainly refers to this. In fact, the practice continues to this day – the tomb of David in Jerusalem is still venerated by many Jews. But there is no record whatsoever of any such veneration of the tomb of Jesus by his disciples – an unthinkable omission, unless there was a very good reason for it.

That reason appears to be the simple fact that Jesus' body was missing from its tomb. There seems to have been no dispute about this at the time – indeed, the rumour of Jesus' resurrection could have been put down without the slightest difficulty by the authorities simply by publicly displaying the corpse of Jesus.

It is of the greatest importance that the New Testament does not contain so much as the slightest trace of an attempt to reconcile belief in Jesus' resurrection with the existence of his corpse in some Palestinian grave. Nor is there any hint – in the New Testament or anywhere else – that the Jewish authorities either produced, or attempted to produce, the corpse of Jesus. Had this been done, the preaching of the early church would have been discredited immediately. But the intriguing fact remains that no such move was made to discredit the first Christians' proclamation of the resurrection and its implications – and the simplest explanation of this remarkable omission is that the corpse was disquietingly absent from its tomb. All the evidence indicates that the tomb was empty on the third day. The controversy at the time concerned not the *fact* of the empty tomb, but the *explanation* of that emptiness.

Matthew records one explanation advanced by one group of critics of Jesus – the disciples had stolen the body at night (Matthew 28:13–15). But it is clear that the disciples believed in a somewhat more exciting explanation – that Jesus had been raised from the dead.

Once more, we must emphasize this point: there can be no doubt that the first disciples *did* believe Jesus had been raised by God. The reports concerning the empty tomb are completely consistent with this belief, and must be regarded as being at least as historically accurate as any other reported event from that time. Our task is simply to account for this belief, and ask whether it is likely to be correct.

Some recent thinkers have argued that the empty tomb is actually irrelevant because it does not prove that the resurrection took place. It is difficult to follow the logic of this argument. It is certainly true that, taken by itself, the empty tomb does not prove that the resurrection took place. What we are talking about, however, is not a *single* piece of evidence but the *cumulative force* of a number of pieces of evidence which combine to give an essentially consistent picture of what happened on the first Easter Day and its significance for believers. If the resurrection did indeed take place, one would expect the tomb to have been empty. It is therefore important to note the unanimous tradition of all four gospels to the effect that this was the case. It certainly does not prove that Christ was raised – but taken in conjunction with other pieces of evidence, it is seen to be of importance in establishing an overall picture of the event of the resurrection.

Thirdly, there are persistent accounts in the New Testament documents of Jesus appearing to his disciples (such as Matthew 28:8–10, 16–20; Luke 24:13–43; John 20:11–29; Acts 1:1–11). Whatever we may make of these accounts, it is clear that the first Christians realized that the same person who had been crucified and buried was very much alive. Although he had unquestionably died, in some way – and the New Testament accounts of the resurrection appearances suggest that those who experienced Christ in this way found it difficult to put their experience into words – he still encountered men and women and made himself known to them. Paul's references to this are of particular importance (1 Corinthians 15:3–8), in that Paul believed it was the *risen* Christ who had appointed him as an apostle. We shall return to the importance of the resurrection for Paul later in this chapter.

Fourthly, we have to account for the transformation of the first Christians and the remarkable advances which Christianity made in the period immediately after Christ's death. It is clear from the gospel accounts of Jesus' betrayal that the disciples were devastated by his arrest and execution. The fact that Peter was moved to deny Jesus at this point is particularly significant (Mark 14:66–72). It is clear that the disciples were demoralized to the point of despair by the betrayal and crucifixion. Indeed, the gospels do not record the presence of any of the leading disciples at Calvary. Mark notes the presence of three women in particular at the scene (Mark 15:40–41), but his attention appears to be mainly directed towards the reaction of the Roman centurion to Jesus' death. Mark also fails to note the presence of the disciples at Christ's burial (Mark 15:42–47). Indeed, Mark appears to go to some lengths to emphasize that the only witnesses present at Jesus' death and burial (Mary Magdalene and Mary the mother of James) were also those who first discovered the empty tomb (Mark 15:40, 47; 16:1–8). John notes that the disciples met secretly in the aftermath of the crucifixion 'for fear of the Jews' (John 20:19).

But this all changes remarkably suddenly. If the accounts of the early church recorded in Acts are anything to go by, the disciples appear to have undergone a remarkable transformation. They were transformed from a band of cowering and demoralized disciples to potential martyrs who proclaimed the resurrection of Jesus with remarkable boldness. An early Christian sermon recorded in Acts makes clear the understanding of what happened underlying this remarkable change:

> This Jesus, delivered up according to the definite plan and fore-knowledge of God, you crucified and killed by the hands of lawless men. But God raised him up, having loosed the pangs of death, because it was not possible for him to be held by it (Acts 2:23–24).

Note the emphasis upon the necessity of the crucifixion – the possibility that it was an accidental end to Jesus' ministry is excluded in favour of the view that this seemingly appalling and senseless event was part of God's intention for Jesus, possessing a deeper meaning and significance.

It is, of course, possible that the disciples were deluded idiots who were content to be martyred for a myth. There is little doubt that many of the early Christians were subjected to various forms of unpleasantness, and some executed, for reasons directly related to their faith. The Book of Revelation, the final (and most enigmatic!) work in the New Testament, appears to have been written with this situation in mind. A similar situation may underlie 1 Peter. In both cases, appeal is made to the resurrection of Jesus as a ground for hope in the face of such opposition, even when death is seen as the inevitable consequence.

Later, the practical results of martyrdom came to be more fully appreciated – the African Christian theologian Tertullian, writing in the early third century, remarked that 'the blood of the martyrs is the seed of the church'. In other words, martyrdom has useful propaganda value.

The early Christians, however, appear to have been content to accept this fate on the basis of another consideration – the belief that those who suffered with Christ would one day be raised from the dead, just as he had been. They may have been completely deluded in this confident expectation – but there is no doubt that they firmly believed in it, and thus force us to account for the origins of their belief. As a piece of circumstantial evidence, it unquestionably points to something or other which gave rise to this belief – and the resurrection of Jesus is totally consistent with it.

Acts also records a remarkable growth in the church at this early stage: a growth which continued after the New Testament period. Early Christianity was not spread at the point of the sword, by force, but through the persuasiveness of its preaching (and Acts may well give us insights into the nature of that preaching). By the early fourth century, Christianity had become so widespread and influential that it was recognized as the official religion of the Roman Empire. From this

point onwards its successes must be attributed at least in part
to its new official status. But before this point it had nothing
to commend it except its beliefs.

Of these beliefs we know that the idea of resurrection was
considered essential and appears to have been a leading
feature of early Christian preaching. Despite hostility on
every side, early Christianity possessed a vitality which kept
it going and kept it spreading. This vitality was unquestionably a reflection of a belief in the resurrection of Jesus. Once
more, it is necessary to note the possibility that the early
Christians were wrong in this belief – although some of the
alternative explanations of the origins of this belief are more
improbable than the idea of resurrection itself! But the fact
still remains that this idea was central to the worship and
preaching of the first Christians, and it remains so to this
day.

Fifthly, we must consider the remarkably exalted understandings of Jesus which became widespread within Christian
circles so soon after his death. Jesus was not venerated as a
dead prophet or rabbi – as we have already seen, he was
worshipped as the living and risen Lord. The use of the word
'Lord' in the New Testament is worth noting, and we shall
discuss it in the next chapter. At some points in the New
Testament, Jesus appears to be explicitly identified with God
himself, and some sort of implicit identification along these
lines is widespread and would become normative in the
following centuries. At several points in the New Testament,
words originally referring to God himself are applied to
Jesus. Two examples are especially interesting. In Romans
10:13 Paul states that 'everyone who calls upon the name of
the Lord [Jesus, in this case] will be saved' – yet the original
of the Old Testament quotation (Joel 2:32) is actually a
statement to the effect that everyone who calls upon the
name of *God* will be saved.

In Philippians 2:10 Paul alters an Old Testament prophecy
to the effect that everyone will one day bow at the name of

God (Isaiah 45:23) to refer to Jesus. Of course, Paul regarded this identification of Jesus and God as perfectly legitimate on the basis of the resurrection. John established the basic practice of referring to Jesus as 'Lord and God' (John 20:28) – a title which Thomas gave to Jesus, according to John, after being convinced that the resurrection really did take place.

Thus Gregory Nazianzen, writing in the fourth century, stated that Christians believed in a 'God who was made flesh and put to death in order that we might live again'. The term *Theotokos* ('Bearer of God', or perhaps 'Mother of God') came to be used to refer to Mary in the fourth century, and was basically an expression of the belief that her child was (in some sense) none other than God himself.

But how could this remarkable transformation in the perceived status of Jesus have come about? He died as a common criminal. But even as a prophet or martyr the most this would merit would be veneration of his tomb (see Matthew 23:29). Of course, we have already noted that there was a problem about Jesus' tomb which was found to be empty so soon after his death. But the point still remains important: why did the early Christians start talking about a dead rabbi as if he were God? And, perhaps even more interesting, why did they start talking about him as if he were *alive*, praying to him, and worshipping him?

Once more, we must note that it is possible that they were the victims of a hysterical delusion which has continued to this day. But there is another explanation: that they believed Jesus to be raised from the dead by God, thus establishing or demonstrating the unique relationship between God and Jesus. And it was on the basis of their understanding of this unique relationship that the early Christians based their views of Jesus.

Sixthly, we must consider the way in which the first Christians worshipped. We know that two sacraments or rites became normative within the church in a remarkably short period, both being witnessed to in the New Testament itself. These are baptism and what is now known variously as the 'breaking of the bread', 'communion' or 'eucharist'. Both reflect a strong belief in the resurrection. Thus Paul states that baptism calls to mind the death and resurrection of Jesus (Romans 6:4–5). It is interesting to note that the early church baptized its converts on Easter Day to bring home fully the significance of the resurrection to the sacrament.

Equally, a strong belief in the resurrection has always led to the eucharist being seen as a celebration of the living presence of Christ in his church, rather than a veneration of a dead teacher. Baptism and eucharist alike are essentially celebrations of Christ's Easter *victory*, rather than solemn memorials of the debacle of Good Friday. The belief that the Jesus who was crucified is now alive and present within his church has exercised an enormous influence over Christian worship down the ages, going back to the earliest of times.

Seventhly, we must consider the Christian experience of Jesus down the ages. This is a very difficult thing to assess, because it is so subjective. However, it is clear that Christians have *experienced* Jesus in such a way that they refuse to speak of him in any way other than that of a living Saviour and Lord. Jesus does not come across as a dead teacher, or a past historical figure, but as a present and living reality.

The experience of Paul with the risen Christ on the road to Damascus (described in Acts 9:1–9; 22:4–16; 26:9–18, and referred to in 1 Corinthians 15:8–9; Galatians 1:11–24) has been paralleled in the Christian experience down the centuries to the present day. Whatever we may make of this fact, the point simply is this: Christians find it easy to believe in the resurrection of Jesus basically because they feel they *know* or *experience* him here and now. This evidence would not stand up for one moment in a court of law but it reminds us that Christianity is grounded in experience and that the

Christian experience of Jesus is consistent with the idea of his resurrection.

In an earlier chapter, we suggested that the gospels were rather like detective novels. In her famous detective novel *The Unpleasantness at the Bellona Club*, Dorothy L. Sayers opens the chapter describing Lord Peter Wimsey's breakthrough in the mystery surrounding the death of General Fentiman with the following words:

> 'What put you on to this poison business?' [Detective Inspector Parker] asked.
>
> 'Aristotle, chiefly,' replied Wimsey. 'He says, you know, that one should always prefer the probable impossible to the improbable possible. It was possible, of course, that the General should have died off in that neat way at the most confusing moment. But how much nicer and more probable that the whole thing had been stage-managed.'

Inevitably, we are faced with a similar dilemma in dealing with the resurrection of Jesus. There are a number of perfectly possible explanations of the evidence we noted above. Jesus may possibly just have fainted on the cross, and revived in the tomb, to wander off into the unknown; the first Christians may possibly have been the victims of hysterical delusions; the 'resurrection' may possibly have been an invention of the disciples to cover up their own theft of Jesus' corpse from the tomb. These are all possibilities – but somehow, they seem terribly implausible. They simply don't have the 'ring of truth' about them. They are 'improbable possibles', to use Wimsey's terms. And so we begin to consider the 'probable impossible' – the astonishing suggestion that Jesus really did rise from the dead, and that this simple assumption more than adequately accounts for the evidence in our possession.

But an objection may well be raised that the resurrection is simply an impossibility, and therefore cannot have happened, no matter what the evidence may be for suggesting that it did. This point is important, and we shall illustrate its fundamental weakness by looking at the famous debate between two German scholars over precisely this point. Ernst Troeltsch, writing at the turn of the present century, argued that what he called the 'principle of analogy' must govern our thinking about Jesus. In other words, we should ask whether present-day analogies exist in the case of the events reported in the gospels. If they do exist, we may conclude that a reasonable foundation has been laid for establishing that these events actually did take place – obviously, it doesn't *prove* that they did take place. To give an example: Jesus was executed by crucifixion. There were countless analogues of the process of crucifixion as a form of execution at the time, for which we have excellent archaeological and literary evidence. The idea of 'execution' still has present-day analogues, although not in the more civilized parts of western Europe. We may therefore conclude that there is a real possibility that Jesus was executed by crucifixion. Now we must establish whether this possibility did, in fact, take place – and on the basis of the evidence available from the gospels, we may conclude with reasonable certainty that it did.

But what if an event recorded in the gospels is without a present-day analogue? To give an example: Jesus was raised from the dead. This is claimed to be a unique event – no one has ever been raised from the dead before (despite the occasional insignificant references to something possibly along the same lines in Egyptian or Nordic mythology, and despite resuscitations [not resurrections to a new kind of life] as with Lazarus and others). No one presently alive has ever witnessed a resurrection – indeed, the Christian claim that Christ's resurrection is unique suggests that this is impossible anyway. Therefore, Troeltsch argued, we must conclude that the resurrection probably did not happen.

It is interesting to reflect on the following point. Let us suppose that something absolutely unique, which has never been repeated, took place about two thousand years ago, in an obscure part of the civilized world. (Perhaps a bloody corpse, fresh from an expert execution, and obviously dead, came back to life?) Accounts of it, ultimately going back to eye-witnesses, were written down shortly afterwards, and preserved to the present day. Would a present-day observer be inclined to believe that the event has actually happened? He would probably not, unconsciously allowing his methods of investigation to dictate his view of what could and what could not have happened. There are excellent reasons for thinking that, on the basis of the methods and presuppositions of some contemporary historians, unique and extraordinary events simply cannot be thought of as ever happening. So what happens if one actually did take place?

Although Troeltsch's point was taken seriously by scholars for several decades, it is now regarded as somewhat old-fashioned. The most important criticism of it to have been made recently is due to the brilliant and greatly respected German theologian Wolfhart Pannenberg. Pannenberg criticized this approach along the following lines. The 'principle of analogy' is basically a useful tool for historical research – but Troeltsch has turned it into a dogmatic view of reality. In other words, Troeltsch is saying that because we have no present-day analogues of something, it simply can't have happened in the first place. A unique event is therefore excluded from the outset, because it doesn't have any parallels today. What Troeltsch is saying is that the resurrection can't have happened, because dead men don't rise. In other words, resurrections don't happen, so the resurrection of Jesus can't have happened. But, as Pannenberg emphasizes, all that Troeltsch is doing is to exclude the resurrection as a possibility altogether, no matter what the evidence in favour of it may be. According to Pannenberg, we should abandon this unjustified dogmatic view of what can happen and what can't, and simply concentrate on the evidence for the resurrection with open minds about its possibility. And, according to Pannenberg, the evidence in favour of the resurrection being a real historical event is decisive. Like Lord Peter Wimsey in Dorothy Sayer's tale, we must abandon our pre-conceived ideas about what can happen and what can't, and be open-minded about the evidence.

Christ, then, was raised from the dead. But so what? We remember the difference between an event and its meaning – what is the *meaning* of the resurrection? The New Testament gives us several answers to this question. First, it shows us how the resurrection was good news *personally* to certain individuals. Secondly, it explores the significance of the resurrection for the identity of Jesus. We begin by looking at the more personal aspects of the resurrection, before considering its second aspect in the following chapter.

The resurrection transformed individuals. John 20:11–18 is an account of how the resurrection was recognized to be good news by Mary Magdalene, who is presented to us as a grieving and distraught individual, convinced that she has lost her Lord for ever: 'They have taken away my Lord, and I do not know where they have laid him' (John 20:13). The moment of recognition, in which Mary suddenly realizes who it is who is addressing her, is often regarded as one of the more tender moments of the New Testament. The moment of recognition, and the simultaneous dawning of hope and joy, are adequate testimony to the personal relevance of the gospel of the resurrection in this case. In the case of Peter, we encounter a betrayer, a failed apostle who denied Christ when he was convinced he would have given his life for the privilege of confessing his name. Peter was called to be an apostle by the lakeside (Luke 5:1–11). The scene of his failure was the 'charcoal fire' (John 18:18) in the courtyard of the High Priest. With great skill, John's gospel draws our attention to the fact that Peter and the disciples' final encounter with the risen Lord incorporates both these elements (John 21:1–19) in a new commissioning of Peter and the disciples by the risen Christ. The symbols of calling and failure are there, reminding them of the past – but the risen

Christ is also there, the symbol of hope, forgiveness and a new beginning, summed up in the new commissioning of the disciples. Peter will not fail to confess Christ again – and, in an aside, we are reminded of the price he finally paid for that confession (John 21:19). Today, in the bread and wine of the eucharistic celebration, we are fed and nourished by the body and blood of the risen Christ, and reminded that the risen Christ is present among us, encountering us, calling us and claiming us as his own.

An illustration may help to bring this point out. The full impact of the horror of the First World War upon the British people can never be fully appreciated by those who didn't go through it themselves. The most appalling carnage and suffering was seen on the battlefields of Flanders, on the banks of the Somme, and elsewhere. And, as people looked back on this war, it was hoped that it would be the war to end all wars – that the death and suffering of so many might not be in vain. A symbol was chosen to express this hope of peace arising from the carnage of war – the poppy. In the blood-drenched ground of Flanders, poppies sprang up – and were seen as symbols of hope, of new life in the face of death. And so the poppy was worn on the anniversary of the ending of the First World War, to remind all of the carnage of war and the hope that sprang up in its aftermath. All too soon, of course, it became clear that this was probably a vain hope.

In many ways, the bread and wine of the eucharist symbolize something very similar to those poppies – life through death, hope in the face of apparent despair. The bread and wine are the poppies of the cross, symbolizing the Christian hope of eternal life in the midst of a world of death and decay, established on the basis of the crucifixion and resurrection of Christ. It is this element of hope – in the Christian sense of a sure and confident expectation that God will raise us up as he once raised Christ – that underlies the eucharistic celebration of Christ's death and resurrection. In the words of George Herbert:

Rise, heart, thy Lord is risen. Sing his praise
Without delays,
Who takes thee by the hand, that thou likewise
With him mayst rise.

The resurrection means that the limitations of space and time are abolished. We do not need to be born again as first-century Palestinians to encounter Christ, in that the risen Christ finds us and calls us, whatever our situation. Christ breaks down historical and cultural barriers – and ultimately the barrier of death itself – precisely because he is risen and alive. For man, death means a severing of relationships, in that he is cut off from those whom he knew and loved. In the case of Jesus, we find that his death had exactly the opposite effect on account of the resurrection – it restored him to fellowship with those whom he loved (Mary Magdalene being a good example) and opened up the possibility of fellowship with those whom (so to speak) he had never known – like us.

Many of us have read the memoirs of dead statesmen. I remember once hearing a recording of some of the wartime speeches of Winston Churchill. As I listened to them, I became conscious of three things. First, that the man had a remarkable grasp of rhetoric, a way of using words to great effect, denied to lesser mortals like myself. Secondly, he was dead, and that I was listening to a voice from the past, preserved only in the form of magnetic imprints. Thirdly, that the situation which he was addressing was no longer of any particular relevance. The Second World War was long since over, and there was no immediate danger of hordes of hostile armies surrounding my room. The Battle of Britain was something I read about in history books, rather than a crucial struggle under way at this very moment, with its outcome uncertain. The contrast with Jesus is obvious. Christians simply cannot think of Jesus as a distant voice from the past, in that he is so obviously experienced as a present reality. Man's situation is more or less the same as it ever has been – confronted with his mortality, he needs a reason for hope and meaning in the face of death and extinction. The resurrection of the one who was crucified, and the assurance that those who suffer with Christ will one day be glorified with him (Romans 8:15–18), is potentially precisely such a reason.

To take this point a little further: all of us, especially those interested in the history of ideas, are only too painfully aware of the way in which intellectual fashions change. Philosophical ideas which were adopted by one generation are often just abandoned (rather than actually disproved) by another. The astonishingly rapid collapse of Hegelianism in Germany in the last century is a case in point. It is almost as if mankind wanders from one set of 'isms' to another, only to turn, dissatisfied, to yet another. Although Christianity can be stated (although not entirely satisfactorily) in terms of philosophical ideas of one sort or another, it is basically about the identity and significance of a *person*.

We emphasized earlier that in Christ, the messenger and the message coincide. When addressing the Christians at Corinth (1 Corinthians 1:17–2:5), Paul emphasized that the gospel was not about human wisdom, but about the power of God demonstrated in the cross of Christ. Despite all the changes in the world of ideas that the last two thousand years have seen, the gospel has not become irrelevant in the way that so many philosophical systems – each of which was modern and relevant in its own day – have done. Why not? Because what is passed down from one generation to another is the experience of the presence of the crucified and risen Christ. One generation may attempt to explain its significance in Hegelian terms, and another in existentialist terms – but the death of Hegelianism, for example, did not bring with it the death of Christianity. Each generation may (and, indeed, must) try to explain the identity and significance of Jesus in ideas or terms which make sense to its contemporaries – but what is passed on from one generation to another is not so much these ideas or terms, but the living reality which lies behind them. To take the resurrection seriously is to realize that the living and risen Christ is – to put it crudely – much bigger than any one generation's apprehension or understanding of him, and that he will be equally really present to future generations, despite differences in culture or intellectual outlook.

Our attention now turns to the New Testament understandings of the identity of Jesus. In what ways did the first Christians understand Jesus? Who did they think he was? We shall consider these questions in the following chapter.

5

The New Testament Witness to the Person of Jesus

The witness of the New Testament to Jesus Christ is complex. At times it explicitly refers to him as God. At others it uses highly suggestive titles to refer to him – Messiah, Son of God, Lord, Saviour and so on. In the present chapter we are going to look at some of these titles and attempt to make sense of them before looking at the most powerful and profound way of thinking about Jesus – that of the Incarnation – in the chapters which follow. But before we do this, we must remember that the New Testament witness to Jesus concerns far more than the titles it uses to refer to him. It concerns the claims which he made, the things which he did, the impact he made on those who encountered him, the worship that was paid to him, and his resurrection from the dead.

We are presented with a complex overall picture and we cannot really isolate fragments of it. The remarkable feature of the New Testament is actually not so much that it refers to Jesus as 'Lord', or that he was worshipped by the early Christians, or that he was raised from the dead – but that *all* these things, and many more besides, are true *of the one and the same man*. These may be seen as the development of perfectly legitimate insights into the identity and significance of Jesus, rather than as inventions or serious distortions of the evidence. The facts about Jesus were, from the beginning, such that it was – sooner or later – appropriate to refer to him in the way that we actually find in the New Testament. There is every reason to suppose that there was a direct, continuous and unbroken line between the historical figure of Jesus of Nazareth and the church's Christological interpretation of his identity and significance. What was it, we must ask, about Jesus that caused the first Christians to speak about him in these ways?

It is clear that the first Christians regarded Jesus as both the source and the object of their religious experience – in other words, their experiences were understood to depend on him and to derive from him. They didn't experience the same sorts of things (such as God) in the same way that Jesus experienced them – they clearly understood their experience of God to derive from Jesus the Lord, and only to make sense when this was realized. The conviction that Jesus was a present and living reality, the source of authentic experience of God, is deeply embedded in the New Testament. Jesus is simply not understood as an example of how we experience God, but as the source of our experience of God – and even as the *object* of our experience of God, so that Jesus may be said to be experienced in the same way as God. This important point illustrates how appallingly inadequate it is to suggest that Jesus relates to Christians in much the same way as a rabbi relates to his disciples, or the founder of a university to his students. Indeed, it is tempting to suggest that those who speak of Jesus in this way have never really experienced the profound and vital impact of Christianity, perhaps overlooking – and certainly minimizing – the emotional aspects of faith in Christ. Certainly Jesus is revered and imitated – to the somewhat limited extent that is possible – but the Christian experience of Jesus far transcends this. Once more, we must pause and reflect upon the impact of the resurrection upon the first Christians, and their understanding of its relevance for their relation to the crucified Jesus.

The complex New Testament witness to Jesus Christ is probably best understood as a gradual drawing out of something which was always there from the beginning. In other words, the first Christians were confronted with something so exciting and novel in the life, death and resurrection of Jesus that they were obliged to employ a whole range of images, terms and ideas to describe it. There was simply no single term available which could capture the richness and profundity of the first Christians' impressions and experience of Jesus. They were thus forced to use a whole variety of terms, one of which might illuminate one aspect of their understanding of him, another of which might illuminate a different aspect – and, taken together, combined to build up an overall picture of Christ. At times they may even have borrowed ideas from paganism to try and build up this picture – for example, it is often thought that John 1:1–18, with its emphasis on the 'Word' (Greek: *logos*), is trying to show that Jesus occupies the same place in the Christian understanding of the world as the idea of the *Logos* occupies in secular Greek philosophy. But this doesn't mean that Christians invented their understanding of Jesus' significance because they happened to read a few textbooks of Stoic philosophy – it just means that they noticed an analogy or parallel, and saw the obvious advantages to be gained by exploiting it to express something which they already knew (and, of course, to make Christianity more understandable to Greek philosophers).

We know that the early Christian church exploded (there is no other word which really describes the impact which it made) into the first–century Mediterranean world. In the course of this astonishingly rapid advance, it encountered both Jewish and Greek cultures. The Jews already knew all about ideas like 'Messiah' and 'Son of God', which made it easy for the Christians to explain their understanding of Jesus to them. It was merely necessary to persuade them that Jesus was indeed the fulfilment of the Old Testament prophecies, the long-promised Messiah. Matthew's gospel seems to have been written with this sort of audience in mind – in an earlier chapter, we noticed how often he points out the parallels between Jesus' ministry and Old Testament prophecies.

In the case of the Greeks, it was more difficult. After all, the Christians could hardly have expected their Greek audience to have read the entire Old Testament before they could have the gospel explained to them. And so they used analogies and ideas which would express their understanding of the identity and significance of Jesus in terms that their Greek readers could understand – Acts 17:16–34 describes Paul's 'Areopagus sermon' at Athens, in which exactly this can be seen happening. Terms like 'Saviour' or 'Redeemer' could be used, which didn't totally depend upon the Old Testament for their meaning. But all that the Christians were doing was expressing something they already knew, something that was already there, in new and different ways, in order to get their message across. The fact that Christianity found it so easy to cross cultural barriers at the time is a remarkable testimony to the effectiveness of the first Christians' attempts to express their beliefs in ways that made sense outside a Jewish context.

Let us begin our examination of some of the titles used by the New Testament to refer to Jesus by looking at the title 'the Christ', or 'the Messiah' – the two are the same, the former being the Greek version, the latter the Hebrew. (The two words are found together in John 1:41.) Thus when Peter recognizes Jesus as 'the Christ, the Son of the living God' (Matthew 16:16), he is identifying Jesus with the long-awaited Messiah. It is, of course, very easy for the modern reader to assume that 'Christ' was Jesus' surname, and to forget that it is actually a title – in other words, 'Jesus the Christ'. The term 'Messiah' literally means 'the anointed one' – in other words, someone who has been anointed with oil. This Old Testament practice indicated that the person anointed in this way was regarded as having been singled out by God as having special powers and functions – thus 1 Samuel 24:6 refers to the king as 'the Lord's anointed'. The basic sense of the word could be said to be 'the divinely appointed King of Israel'. As time passed, the term gradually came to refer to a deliverer, himself a descendant of David, who would restore Israel to the golden age she enjoyed under the rule of David.

It must be remembered that at the time of Jesus' ministry, Palestine was occupied and administered by Rome. There was intense nationalist feeling at the time, and this appears to have become linked with the expectation of the coming of the Messiah. For many, the Messiah would be the deliverer who expelled the Romans from Israel and restored the line of David. It is clear that Jesus refused to see himself as Messiah in this sense. At no point in his ministry do we find any violence against Rome suggested or condoned, nor do we find even an explicit attack on the Roman administration. Jesus' attacks are directed primarily against his own people. Thus after his triumphal entry into Jerusalem (Matthew 21:8–11), which gives every indication of being a deliberate messianic demonstration or gesture, Jesus immediately evicts the merchants from the temple (Matthew 21:12–13).

Interestingly, Jesus was not prepared to accept the title 'Messiah' in the course of his ministry. Mark's gospel should be read carefully to note this point. When Peter acclaims Jesus as Messiah – 'You are the Christ!' – Jesus immediately tells him to keep quiet about it (Mark 8:29–30). It is not clear what the full significance of the 'Messianic secret' is. Why should Mark emphasize that Jesus did not make an explicit claim to be the Messiah, when he was so clearly regarded as such by so many? Perhaps the answer lies later in Mark's gospel, when he recounts the only point at which Jesus explicitly acknowledges his identity as the Messiah. When Jesus is led, as a prisoner, before the High Priest, he admits to being the Messiah (Mark 14:61–62). In other words, once violent or political action of any sort is no longer possible, Jesus reveals his identity. Jesus was indeed the deliverer of the people of God – but not, it would seem, in any political sense of the term. The misunderstandings associated with the term, particularly in Zealot circles, appear to have caused Jesus to play down the messianic side of his mission.

It is also clear that the Jews did not expect their Messiah to be executed as a common criminal. It is worth noting that, immediately after Peter acknowledges Jesus as the Messiah, Jesus begins to explain to his disciples that he must suffer, be rejected by his own people and be killed (Mark 8:29–31) – hardly an auspicious end to a messianic career. Indeed, Paul made it clear to the Corinthian Christians that the very idea of 'a crucified Messiah' (or 'a crucified Christ') was scandalous to a Jew (1 Corinthians 1:23). From a very early stage, it is clear that Christians recognized a link between Jesus' messiahship and the destiny of the mysterious 'Suffering Servant':

> He was despised and rejected by men; a man of sorrows, and acquainted with grief; and as one from whom men hide their faces he was despised, and we esteemed him not. Surely he has borne our griefs and carried our sorrows; yet we esteemed him stricken, smitten by God, and afflicted. But he was wounded for our transgressions, he was bruised for our iniquities; upon him was the chastisement that made us whole, and with his stripes we are healed. All we like sheep have gone astray; we have turned every one to his own way; and the Lord has laid upon him the iniquity of us all (Isaiah 53:3–6).

A second title which claims our attention is 'Lord' (Greek: *kyrios*). The word is used in two main senses in the New Testament. First, it is used as a polite title of respect, particularly when addressing someone. When I write a letter to my bank manager, beginning 'Dear Sir', I am not for one moment implying that he has been knighted – I am just being polite. Similarly, when a pupil addresses his teacher as 'Sir', he is also being polite. The same principle applies in several passages in the New Testament. Thus when Martha speaks to Jesus and addresses him as 'Lord' (John 11:21), she is probably – although not necessarily – merely treating Jesus with proper respect.

Of infinitely greater importance, however, are the frequent passages in the New Testament in which Jesus is referred to as 'the Lord'. The confession that 'Jesus is Lord' (Romans 10:9; 1 Corinthians 12:3) was clearly regarded by Paul as a convenient statement of the essential feature of the gospel. Christians are those who 'call upon the name of the Lord' (Romans 10:13; I Corinthians 1:2). But what is implied by this affirmation? It is clear that there was a tendency in first-century Palestine to use the word 'Lord' (Greek: *kyrios*; Aramaic: *mare*) to designate a divine being, or at the very least a figure who is decidedly more than just human, in addition to its function as a polite or honorific title for a person of importance. But our attention is particularly claimed by the use of this Greek word *kyrios* to translate the four letters used to refer to God in the Old Testament.

The Old Testament writers were reluctant to refer to God directly, and on occasions where it was necessary to make reference to God, they tended to use a cipher of four letters (often referred to as the 'Tetragrammaton'). This group of letters, which lies behind the English Authorized Version's references to God as 'Jehovah', and the Jerusalem Bible's references to God as 'Yahweh', was used to represent the sacred name of God. When the Old Testament scriptures were translated from Hebrew into Greek, the word *kyrios* was used to translate the sacred name of God. Thus Josephus tells us that the Jews refused to call the Roman Emperor *kyrios*, because they regarded this name as reserved for God alone.

It is therefore important to notice that the New Testament on occasion transfers an Old Testament reference to 'the Lord' (in other words, God) to 'the Lord Jesus'. Perhaps the most striking example of this tendency may be seen by comparing Joel 2:32 with Acts 2:21. Joel refers to a crucial period in the history of the people of God, in which the Spirit of God will be poured out upon all men (Joel 2:28). On this 'great and terrible day of the Lord' (that is, God) (Joel 2:31), 'everyone who calls on the name of the Lord will be saved' (Joel 2:32) – in other words, everyone who calls on the name of God will be saved. This prophecy is alluded to in Acts (2:17–21), in the context of the day of Pentecost, ending with the assertion (Acts 2:21) that 'everyone who calls on the name of the Lord will be saved'. It is then made clear, in what follows, that the 'Lord' in question is none other than 'Jesus of Nazareth', whom God has made 'both Lord and Christ' (Acts 2:36).

A further interesting example may be found in the use made of Isaiah 45:23 in Philippians 2:10–11. According to Isaiah, 'the Lord' (that is, God) states that 'every knee shall bow' to him. Paul, possibly taking up a tradition going back to an earlier stage, identifies 'the Lord' as Jesus in the following passage:

> Therefore God has highly exalted him and bestowed on him the name which is above every name, that at the name of Jesus every knee should bow ... and every tongue confess that Jesus Christ is Lord, to the glory of God the Father (Philippians 2:9–11).

A further example is to be found in Hebrews 1:10, which alters the reference of Psalm 102:25 from God to Jesus. This practice of transferring from one Lord (God) to another (Jesus) is known to have infuriated Jews at the time. Thus in the second-century dialogue between Trypho the Jew and Justin Martyr, Trypho complains that Christians have 'hijacked' passages referring to God in order to refer them to Christ. There was, of course, no suggestion that there were two 'Lords' (in other words, two Gods) – simply that Jesus had to be regarded as having a status at least equal to that of God, which demanded that he be addressed and worshipped as God. The use of the term 'Lord' to refer to Jesus may therefore be seen as a recognition of his exalted status, arising from his resurrection.

A further title used by the New Testament to refer to Jesus is 'Son of God'. In the Old Testament, the term is occasionally used to refer to angelic or supernatural persons (Job 38:7; Psalms 82:6; Daniel 3:25). Messianic texts in the Old Testament refer to the coming Messiah as the 'Son of God' (2 Samuel 7:12–14; Psalm 2:7). The New Testament use of the term seems to mark a development of its Old Testament meaning, with an increased emphasis upon its exclusiveness. Although all men are sons of God in some sense of the word, Jesus is *the* Son of God. Paul distinguishes between Jesus as the *natural* Son of God and believers as *adopted* sons – their relationship to God is quite different from Jesus' relationship to him, even though both may be referred to as 'sons of God'. Similarly, in 1 John, Jesus is referred to as the Son, while believers are designated as 'children'. There is something quite distinct about Jesus' relation to God as expressed in the title 'Son of God'.

The New Testament understanding of Jesus' relationship to God, expressed in the Son-Father relationship, takes a number of forms. First, we note that Jesus directly addresses God as 'Father', with the very intimate Aramaic word 'Abba' being used (Matthew 6:9; 11:25–26; 26:42; Mark 14:36; Luke 23:34,46). Secondly, it is clear from a number of passages that the evangelists regard Jesus as the Son of God, or that Jesus treats God as his father, even if this is not stated explicitly (Mark 1:11; 9:7; 12:6; 13:32; 14:61, 62; 15:39). Thirdly, John's gospel is permeated with the Father-Son relationship (John 5:16–27; 17:1–26), with a remarkable emphasis upon the identity of will and purpose of the Father and Son, indicating how close the relationship between Jesus and God was understood to be by the first Christians. At every level in the New Testament – in the words of Jesus himself, or in the impression which was created among the first Christians – Jesus is clearly understood to have a unique and intimate relationship to God, which the resurrection demonstrated publicly (Romans 1:3, 4).

We could continue this examination of the various titles which the New Testament employs to refer to Jesus, to illustrate the many facets of its complex witness to his identity and significance. There is, however, a danger that by doing this we may miss seeing the wood for the trees – in other words, we will fail to see that these titles, together with the New Testament accounts of the impact Christ had upon those whom he encountered, build up to give a pattern. It is clear that the New Testament witnesses to Jesus as the embodiment of all God's promises, witnessed to in the Old Testament, brought to fulfilment and fruition. The statements made about Jesus may be broadly listed under two classes. First, we have statements about Jesus' *function* – statements about what God has done for man in Jesus. Secondly, we have statements about Jesus' *identity* – who he is. The two are, of course, closely connected. Just as a collection of pieces of a jigsaw puzzle build up to give a pattern which no single piece can show on its own, so the New Testament 'Christological titles' build up to give an overall picture which no single title can adequately disclose. Taken collectively, they build up into a rich, deep and powerfully persuasive portrait of Christ as the divine Saviour and Lord who continues to exercise an enormous influence over and appeal to mankind.

What we are going to do now is to examine one way of looking at Jesus, of making sense of him, which has proved particularly helpful and illuminating, and greatly influenced the Christian church down the ages.

6

The Incarnation: The Doctrine

Jesus was a man. Of that, the New Testament leaves us in no doubt. He was thirsty, he was tired, he suffered and he died. It also leaves us in no doubt that he was more than a man. The question is: how are we to make sense of the manner in which Jesus was more than just a man? The approach which we are going to consider in the following chapters is summarized in the prologue to John's gospel (John 1:1–18), and culminates in the following remarkable statement: 'The Word became flesh and dwelt among us, full of grace and truth; we have beheld his glory, glory as of the only Son from the Father, full of grace and truth' (John 1:14). The *Word* (the term used for one who is living, imperishable, creative and divine) *became* (in other words, entered into human history) *flesh* (the term used for what is creaturely, perishable, finite, mortal and human). The idea of 'incarnation' simply means God taking on flesh, humbling himself to take upon himself the entire experience of existence as man in all the conditions of humanity. The one who was there from the beginning, the one who was God, became man. As one of the better-known Christmas carols states:

> Veiled in flesh the Godhead see,
> Hail the incarnate Deity!
> Pleased as man with man to dwell,
> Jesus our Emmanuel!

The full force of this idea, its meaning for our understanding of God and ourselves, will become clear in the following chapter. In the present chapter, we are going to ask whether this idea is a reasonable summary of the New Testament evidence concerning Jesus, and look at the ways in which the Christian church has tried to express it.

As we saw in an earlier chapter, the resurrection exercized a decisive influence upon Christian thinking concerning the identity and significance of Jesus. The theme of the risen life pervades the New Testament, and governs much of the early Christian proclamation. Thus Paul states that the resurrection established that Jesus was the Son of God (Romans 1:3–4). But did Jesus *become* the Son of God at his resurrection, or did the resurrection *disclose* something which had always been true? Did the resurrection change Jesus' status, or did it just make clear what that status had always been?

It is clear from the New Testament that Jesus was regarded as having the same status disclosed by his resurrection (in other words, his being Son of God) in his lifetime. Thus Paul clearly regards Jesus as having this status at the time of his death, speaking of the 'Son of God, who loved me and gave himself for me' (Galatians 2:20). The Synoptic Gospels indicate that Jesus enjoyed this status at least from the time of the beginning of his ministry (Mark 1:11). At some points it even seems to be suggested that Jesus possessed this divine status from the beginning of time (John 1:1–14; Philippians 2:6–11; Colossians 1:15–20). At the very least, we may say that the New Testament indicates that there never was a time in his life that he was not already what the resurrection disclosed him to be – the Son of God. In other words, the resurrection demonstrated or proved Jesus' divine status in his lifetime, the clue to his identity and significance which clinched the case for his claim to a unique relationship to God. Let us look at some ways in which the New Testament expresses the divinity of Jesus.

In an earlier chapter, we noted the difference between a *functional* and an *ontological* Christology. A functional Christology is basically a way of thinking about Jesus which is primarily concerned with establishing what Jesus *did* – his 'function', to put it crudely. An ontological Christology is primarily concerned with establishing who Jesus *is* – his identity. Of course, it is obvious that these two ways of thinking about Jesus are virtually the same in terms of their practical results. If Jesus *is* God, then he *acts as God and for* God. And if Jesus *acts as God and for* God, then to all intents and purposes he *is* God. But there is a difference, and it is important to note it at this point. The New Testament writers seem to have begun their reflection concerning the identity and significance of Jesus by reflecting on what he did for man, and then gone on to ask who Jesus must be if he is able to act in this way. Of course, there are cases in which direct statements are made about his identity – a good example is the one we've just been looking at in which Jesus is recognized as being the Son of God on account of the resurrection. But what did Jesus *do*? And what does it tell us about him? There is, it must be emphasized, no tension between 'functional' and 'ontological' Christologies in the New Testament – rather, there seems to be an obvious progress from the functional to ontological in the New Testament. The first Christians found themselves obliged to speak of Jesus in divine terms, or at least terms which implied divinity, and thus were obliged to go on from there and think through the consequences of these ways of speaking about Jesus for their understanding of the relationship of Jesus to God. Let us look at some important New Testament statements on such matters.

1. Jesus saves

In the third part of this book we shall be exploring this theme in more detail, looking at some of the questions which it raises. For example, what does 'save' mean? And how is 'salvation' related to Jesus' life, death and resurrection? However, we can make a very important statement even at this earlier stage: *only God can save!* This great theme is echoed throughout the Old Testament. Israel is reminded time and time again that she cannot save herself, nor can she be saved by the idols of the nations round about her. It is the Lord, and the Lord alone, who will save:

> Who declared it of old? Was it not I, the Lord? And there is no other god besides me, a righteous God and a Saviour; there is none besides me. Turn to me and be saved, all the ends of the earth! (Isaiah 45:21–22).

In the full knowledge that it was God alone who was Saviour, that it was God alone who could save, the first Christians had no hesitation in affirming that Jesus was Saviour, that Jesus could save. Perhaps it is worth remembering how the fish came to be a symbol of faith to the early Christians – the five letters spelling out 'fish' in Greek came to represent the slogan 'Jesus Christ, Son of God, Saviour'. In the New Testament, Jesus saves his people from their sins (Matthew 1:21); only in his name is there salvation (Acts 4:12); he is the 'pioneer of . . . salvation' (Hebrews 2:10); he is the 'Saviour, who is Christ the Lord' (Luke 2:11). In these affirmations and countless others, Jesus is understood to *function as God*, doing something which, properly speaking, only God can do.

2. Jesus is worshipped

Within the Jewish context within which the first Christians operated, it was God and God alone who was to be worshipped. As St Paul reminded the Christians at Rome, there was a constant danger that men would worship creatures, when they ought to be worshipping their creator (Romans 1:23). We have already noted the fact that the early Christian church worshipped Christ as God – a practice which is clearly reflected even in the New Testament. Thus 1 Corinthians 1:2 suggests that Christians are those who 'call on the name of our Lord Jesus Christ', using language which reflects the Old Testament formulas for worshipping or adoring God (Genesis 4:26; 13:4; Psalms 105:1; Jeremiah 10:25; Joel 2:32). Jesus is clearly understood to *function* as God, in that he is an object of worship. Within the strict monotheism of the Jewish context within which this worship took place, it is clear that an important statement concerning Jesus' identity and significance is being made.

3. Jesus reveals God

'He who has seen me has seen the Father' (John 14:9). These remarkable words, so characteristic of John's gospel, emphasize the belief that the Father speaks and acts in the Son – in other words, that God is revealed in and by Jesus. The Christian claim that God is most fully and authentically revealed in the face of Jesus Christ is simply a summary statement of the kaleidoscope of New Testament descriptions of the intimate relation between the Father and the Son, between God and Jesus. To have seen Jesus is to have seen the Father – in other words, Jesus is understood, once more, to *function* as God.

4. Jesus represents God

One of the great New Testament themes is that the promises of the Old Testament are fulfilled in the coming of Christ. The promises made by God to his people are seen to have been honoured. But it is clear that the New Testament also contains promises, made by Jesus himself on behalf of God. For example, at the heart of the proclamation of the gospel as we find it in John's gospel lie the great promises of salvation: 'He who believes has eternal life' (John 6:47); 'He who eats my flesh and drinks my blood has eternal life, and I will raise him up on the last day' (John 6:54). According to this gospel, Jesus makes promises on behalf of God. In many respects we may see this as a statement to the effect that Jesus is the plenipotentiary, the authorized representative, of God. This idea is expressed particularly well by the Hebrew concept of the *shaliach* ('plenipotentiary'). When a king sends his *shaliach* to negotiate with someone, that *shaliach* is empowered to act on his behalf – to enter into agreements, to make promises, and so on. Although the king is not himself physically present in these negotiations, to all intents and purposes he might just as well be. The promises made are made on his behalf and will be honoured by him. It is important to notice how often we find reference in John's gospel to the total unity of purpose of Father and Son (John 17:20–25): the Son is sent by the Father (John 6:57; 17:3), and acts on behalf of the Father (John 5:30). Jesus is clearly understood to make such promises on behalf of God, and at the desire of God, and is thus unquestionably understood as *functioning as God and for God* in this respect. Jesus functions as God's *shaliach*, his plenipotentiary representative, in whom and through whom God has pledged himself to act.

We could go on and consider other New Testament understandings of the manner in which Jesus' function and identity are closely inter-related. But it will be clear, on the basis of our discussion so far, that the New Testament at the very least understands Jesus to *act as God and for God* in every area of crucial relevance to Christianity. In short, we must – in the words of a first-century writer – learn to 'think about Jesus as we do about God' (2 Clement 1:1–2). We are thus in a position to take the crucial step which underlies all Christian thinking on the incarnation – that, as Jesus *acts as God and for God in every context of importance*, we should conclude that, for all intents and purposes, *Jesus is God*. Thus when we worship Jesus, we worship God; when we know Jesus, we know God; when we hear the promises of

Jesus, we hear the promises of God; when we encounter Jesus, we encounter none other than the living God. The idea of the incarnation is the climax of Christian reflection upon the mystery of Christ – the recognition that Jesus revealed God; that Jesus represented God; that Jesus speaks as God and for God; that Jesus acted as God and for God; that Jesus *was* God.

Let us return once more to the resurrection. We have already seen that the New Testament recognizes that Jesus was always what the resurrection disclosed him to be. The resurrection established his divine status as Son of God. But where did this status come from? It is at this point that the close relationship between the resurrection and incarnation becomes clear. If Jesus Christ always possessed his unique status, that status must be traced back to his birth, and even further. The incarnation may thus be seen as the logical conclusion of Christian thinking concerning the significance of the resurrection.

Recently there has been some discussion about the logical order of the incarnation and resurrection. One of the disadvantages of not being God is that we see things the wrong way round, looking at things from man's standpoint rather than God's. The order in which things actually exist (the 'order of being' as it is sometimes called) is usually exactly the opposite of the order in which we come to know about them (the 'order of knowing'). We come to *know* about Christ's divinity through the resurrection, and as a result we arrive at the idea of the incarnation. So we could say that the resurrection comes before the incarnation in the 'order of knowing'. But it will be obvious that, once we know about the incarnation, we realize that it must take precedence over the resurrection in the 'order of being'. We could summarize this by saying that Christ *was* divine before the resurrection *discloses* that he is divine. But this argument is not particularly important: all that we need to note here is that there is a very close relationship between the incarnation and resurrection.

The problem that the Christian church had to deal with now was simply this: how can Jesus be both God and man? We have already seen the thinking which lay behind this conclusion – the problem was to make sense of it! The first four or five centuries saw this question being debated at great length throughout the Christian world. In many respects the debates are of little interest, concerning technical matters of Greek philosophy of little relevance for today. But they are important in one respect – they show how well aware the church was that the gospel itself was at stake in these debates. For the early fathers, Jesus had to be both God and man if salvation was to be a possibility. If Jesus was not God, he could not save; If Jesus was not man, man could not be saved. The affirmation that Jesus was both God and man came to be seen as a means of safeguarding the gospel proclamation of the redemption of mankind in Christ. The early Christians were actually far more interested in *defending* this insight, rather than trying to *explain* it! We must never fall into the trap of suspecting that the fathers thought that they were explaining how Jesus could be both God and man – it is clear that they were simply trying to find ways of making sense of a *mystery*, something which in the end defied explanation. But it was no mystery invented just to give bishops or theologians something to do with their spare time – it was the central mystery of the Christian faith, upon which Christianity would stand or fall. To illustrate this point, let us leave the first five centuries of the Christian era behind for a moment, and move to a very different situation – Berlin in the early nineteenth century.

Like many people at the time, Friedrich Schleiermacher, one of the more important Christian thinkers of the last two centuries, found the 'two natures doctrine' (the doctrine that Jesus was both God and man) rather heavy going. On the one hand, it seemed very difficult to understand; on the other hand, it seemed to him that something very much like it was necessary. Why? Let us follow his reasoning through. Let us agree that Christians believe that man is saved only through Jesus Christ. That is a rather bald summary of the many statements of the New Testament on the matter, but it is good enough for our purposes. What does this actually imply? The first point that Schleiermacher makes is this. It is obvious that Jesus is a man. That point does not really need to be emphasized, but it is a good point to start our thinking from. But if he is *just* a man, like all other men, we find ourselves faced with a problem. That means he shares man's need for redemption, so he cannot possibly redeem us. There must be some essential difference between Jesus and man if Jesus is indeed to be our redeemer. After all, Christianity has always insisted that Jesus is the solution to man's problem, rather than part of that problem!

Perhaps we can avoid this problem by dropping the idea that Jesus is man altogether, and simply state that he is God. But then he has no point of contact with those who need redemption. How can he relate to them? There must, then, be some point of difference between Christ and God which allows Christ to make contact with those whom he is meant to redeem. And so we eventually move towards the recognition that Jesus must be God *and* man if he is to redeem man. This simply states the basic principle which lies behind the idea of the incarnation.

We could develop the same idea along different lines. Let us suppose that we have two people – let us call them 'A' and 'B'. A and B enjoy a close relationship, which breaks down completely over some misunderstanding. A is convinced that it is the fault of B, and B is sure that A is in the wrong. So strongly do they hold their views that they refuse to speak to each other. The situation is, unfortunately, all too familiar from everyday experience – whether it is a matter of personal relationships, or industrial relations. We all know situations where this has happened, and may even have been unfortunate enough to have been involved with them our-selves. But how can the situation be resolved? How can A and B become reconciled? It is clear that the situation demands a *mediator*, a *go-between*. Let us reflect on the qualifications such a mediator might need.

It will be obvious that the best mediator or go-between is someone whom both A and B know and respect, but who will be impartial. Let us call this mediator 'C'. C must repre-sent A to B, and B to A. He must not be identified with either A or B, yet he must have points of contact with both if he is to be accepted. This situation is familiar to us all – it's just a question of working out who C must be. To give an example: late Victorian novels often portray a crisis arising between a father and his son, with the mother acting as the mediator between them. Although she is not identical with either father or son, she has relationships with both of them which establish her credentials as a go-between. She is close enough to both of them to represent them both, and yet sufficiently different from them both to prevent her being identified with either. The relevance of this little digression for our understanding of the identity of Jesus Christ will be obvious.

The idea of Jesus being the one and only go-between or mediator between God and man is deeply ingrained in the New Testament. 'For there is one God, and there is one mediator between God and men, the man Christ Jesus' (1 Timothy 2:5). St Paul talks about God 'reconciling' us to himself through Jesus Christ (2 Corinthians 5:18–19). What is particularly interesting is that St Paul uses the same Greek word to refer to the restoration of the relationship between God and man which he had used earlier to refer to the restoration of the relationship between a man and his wife who had fallen out (1 Corinthians 7:10–11). Christ is under-stood to act as the mediator or go-between in restoring the relation between God and man to what it once was. And now we can start applying the ideas we discussed in the previous paragraph. This mediator must represent God to man, and man to God. He must have points of contact with both God and man, and yet be distinguishable from them both. And so on. In short, the traditional idea of the incarnation, which expresses the belief that Jesus is both God and man, portrays Jesus as the perfect mediator between God and man.

How, then, may the idea that Jesus is God be *understood*? The exhaustive discussion in the first five centuries of the precise relationship between Christ, God and man was brought to an end by the Council of Chalcedon (A.D. 451). Just as the chairman of a committee finally feels obliged to bring a debate to an end when all the issues appear to have been raised and exhaustively discussed (only to be raised again!), so the Council of Chalcedon brought the debate within the early church on the identity of Jesus Christ to an end. Over five hundred bishops met to hammer out an agreement which would do justice to the various points which had been raised during the debate. The Christian church in Alexandria (in modern-day Egypt) had laid stress upon the importance of the divinity of Christ, whereas the church in Antioch (in modern-day Turkey) had laid much greater emphasis upon the humanity of Christ. All sorts of theories had been put forward to explain the way in which God and man were united in Christ. Which would the Council adopt?

What the Council actually said is very significant. It didn't lay down one specific way of thinking about the relationship between Jesus, God and man. It stated that it was necessary to regard Jesus Christ as fully divine and fully human. In doing this, the Council was simply restating what was widely agreed within the church: that if Jesus was not God, he was of no relevance to any thought about God and eternal life; that if he was not man, he was irrelevant to any experience of human life. It merely restated a crucially important insight – it didn't explain it, or lay down some specific way of making sense of it. But this was all that the Council wanted to do – to ider⸴ ⸴⸴ the essential point at issue.

The Council of Chalcedon was content to reaffirm a fact without attempting to interpret it – and it was wise to do so. Interpretations vary from one age to another, depending upon the time and place. Platonism might be used to interpret the incarnation in third-century Alexandria, Aristotelianism in thirteenth-century Paris, and Hegelianism in nineteenth-century Berlin. But Chalcedon attempted to safeguard an essential fact which could be interpreted in terms of ideas which make sense at any particular point in history, provided these explanations do not deny or explain away any part of the fact. Every explanation must, in the final analysis, be recognized to be inadequate, and Chalcedon merely stated with great clarity what the essential fact which required explanation and interpretation was: Jesus really is both God and man. So long as Jesus was recognized as being both God and man, all was well. So long as man knows that he really does encounter God, and not some demi-god or deluded egomaniac, in Jesus, he knows that Jesus has a unique position in relation to both God and man, and may base his faith upon it. So long as he knows that in Jesus he really does encounter a man, he may rest assured that God is involved in human history and experience – and, specifically, in his own history and experience.

To make this point absolutely clear, the Council used a technical term already well established by this time. This is the term which is usually translated into English as 'of one substance' or 'of one being'. Jesus is 'of one substance' with God, just as he is 'of one substance' with man. In other words, Jesus is the *same* as God; it really is God himself whom we encounter in Jesus, and not some messenger sent from God.

In the early church there was a remarkably heated debate over two Greek words which differed only by one letter.

One means 'of a similar substance' (*homoiousios*), the other means 'of the same substance' (*homoousios*). We could translate them more simply as 'being like' and 'being the same as'. In his famous book *The Decline and Fall of the Roman Empire* Gibbon pointed out that never before had so much fuss been made over a single letter of the alphabet. But there is all the difference in the world between the two ideas. Let us take the idea of Jesus being 'similar to' God. That means that in Jesus we encounter someone who is like God in some way. It isn't God himself whom we encounter, but his surrogate or representative. God sends his troubleshooter and keeps out of things himself. God remains aloof from human history and human experience – he experiences us at second hand, and we experience him at second hand. How unsatisfactory this would be. Imagine having to communicate with someone we knew and loved through third parties all the time! No human personal relationship can work like that. God does not know what it is like to be frail, weak and mortal – in short, he does not know what it is like to be man, like ourselves. We can only approach God as someone whom we know indirectly, and who knows us indirectly.

At Chalcedon, the church opted conclusively for a different understanding of the relation of Jesus and God. In Jesus we encounter God at first hand, directly. To encounter the risen Christ is to encounter none other than the living and loving God. To put this in a dangerously crude way: God knows what it is like to be human. Although only a single letter separates *homoiousios* ('being like God') from *homoousios* ('being the same as God'), a world separates the views of Jesus which they represent. In English, the difference might be brought out by saying the former corresponds to 'Jesus is good' and the latter to 'Jesus is God'. Chalcedon made no attempt to explain the mystery with which we are confronted as Christians, and we totally misrepresent and misunderstand it if we think it did – it just identified the central point at stake, and made crystal clear the Christian point of view.

To many, the Chalcedonian definition is unspeakably tedious and practically unintelligible. It reads like a legal document, rather than a statement conveying the excitement and vitality of faith. It is, of course, the job of a preacher to translate Chalcedon into everyday language. In the following chapter we're going to do this. But a few thoughts at this stage might be helpful. Chalcedon simply states in a form of a definition what the first five centuries of Christian reflection on the New Testament had already established – the sorts of things which we have been discussing in this chapter. It isn't an arbitrary invention, the product of confused minds, but an attempt to sum up a long and important debate and declare its result. Although turgid and unexciting to read, the defintion established the basis upon which faith depends – the *sine qua non*.

No one would dream of confusing a marriage certificate with a marriage – yet the certificate declares the essential basis upon which a marriage rests. It is the starting point for building and development, not an end in itself. Chalcedon defines the point from which we start – the recognition that, in the face of Christ, we see none other than God himself. That is a starting point, not an end. But we must be sure of our starting point, the place at which we begin, if the result is to be reliable. Chalcedon claims to have established that starting point, and whatever difficulties we may find with its turgid language and outdated expressions, the basic ideas which it lays down are clear and crucial, and are obviously a legitimate interpretation of the New Testament witness to Jesus Christ. But now we must ask: what happens when we go on from this starting point? What does the incarnation tell us about God and about ourselves? What does it tell us about the nature of God and the destiny of man? In short, what is the cash value of the incarnation? Let us go on and see.

7

The Incarnation: Its Significance

Jesus is God – that is the basic meaning of the incarnation. It is a remarkably profound and exciting idea which has enormous consequences for the way in which we think about ourselves and about God. In this chapter we are going to 'unpack' the meaning of the belief that Jesus is both God and man. Some of the ideas it involves are simple, others are more complex. Let us begin with a simple idea.

What is God like? This is a crucial question and we shall be exploring it further in a moment. But first we need to ask a penetrating question: *how* do we know what God is like in the first place? Before we start thinking about the results, we need to think about the means we will use to get them. When the Christian speaks of God, he means God as he has been revealed in Jesus Christ – the God who became incarnate. What can we say about God? He is immortal, invisible, infinite, and so on – but that is hardly very informative. All that we are actually saying is that God is *not* mortal, God is *not* visible, God is *not* finite. While all this may well be true, it is hardly very exciting or interesting. What can we say *positively* about God? It is here that the incarnation establishes a crucial principle: God is Christlike. These three simple words can totally alter our way of thinking about God. Let us look at an example to bring out the importance of this principle.

What can we say about the love of God for man? We could say that it is infinite, boundless, beyond human telling, and so on – but, once more, all that we have done is to speak of it *negatively*, explaining what it is *not*. In fact, we are virtually saying that, whatever the love of God may be like, we can't say anything about it. But the love of God is a rather import- ant and exciting aspect of Christianity, something which we would clearly very much like to be able to talk about! Surely we can say something clear, intelligible, positive and exciting about it – unless we are doomed to have to keep quiet about it for ever! On the basis of the incarnation, we may make a very positive and simple statement about the love of God for man. The love of God is like the love of a man who lays down his life for his friends (John 15:13). Immediately, we are given a picture, an image, drawn from human experience – something concrete and tangible, something we can visual- ize and relate to. A picture is worth a thousand words – and in the picture of a man laying down his life, giving his very being, for someone whom he loves, we have a most power- ful, striking and moving statement of the full extent of the love of God for sinful man. We can talk about the love of God in terms of our own experience, and supremely in terms of the tender image of Jesus Christ trudging to Calvary, there to die for those whom he loved. It is a moving, poig- nant and deeply evocative image which we can easily imagine and identify with – in short, it is a statement about the love of God which speaks to us, which appeals to us and which brings home exactly what the love of God is like. No longer need we be at a loss for words to speak about God. We are given a handle to attach to God in order that we may get hold of him. One of the early church fathers, Origen, com- pared the incarnation to a small statue – a scaled-down model of the real thing which allows us to discern its features more clearly.

We may go further than this. Until Christ came, every image of God may be said to have been an idol – something which we ourselves constructed and worshipped. In Christ we are given an image of God – something we can visualize, imagine in our minds, and relate to. Without the death of Christ, there is every danger that our conception of the love of God will be soft and sentimental. But the cross brings home the deep relationship of severity and kindness, already known to every parent, which is so characteristic of God's dealings with us. The appalling cost of forgiveness to God is shown in the cross. God does not simply say, 'Never mind,' to the sinner, pretending that sin never happened or that it is of no significance. We wouldn't accept that concept of forgiveness for ourselves, so why should we force it on God? True forgiveness involves facing and recognizing the great pain and distress caused by the offence – a process for which the cross is perhaps the most powerful illustration known. The love of God for his people is expressed, not in a soft and sentimental way, but in the context of the seriousness of God's hatred for sin. The cross sets forward the full and tremendous cost of *real* forgiveness – a forgiveness in which the full seriousness of sin is met and dealt with, in order that love may triumph. The cross confronts us with the knowledge that man's sin wounds God to the heart, causing more hurt than we can ever imagine. Yet God offers man forgiveness – a *real*, if painful, forgiveness in which all is faced and all is forgiven in order that man may go forth into eternal life with his God. Recognition of sin is a humiliating, painful and healing process. The incarnation helps us to realize that God humbled himself to meet us, and that we too must humble ourselves if we are to meet him.

The incarnation makes God tangible. It helps us think about God. It is quite astonishing how the question, 'Is Christ divine?' is discussed as if we had an excellent idea about what God was like, while Christ himself remained something of an enigma. But exactly the opposite is so obviously the case! Christ confronts us through the gospel narratives and through experience, whereas we have no clear vision of God. As John's gospel reminds us: 'No one has ever seen God; the only Son, who is in the bosom of the Father, has made him known' (John 1:18). God is Christlike – in other words, we learn to think of God as we see him in Christ. For the Christian, it is Christ who provides us with the basis of the most reliable knowledge of God available.

We could further unpack the meaning of the incarnation by thinking about two pieces of glass. The first is a window. Suppose you are in a room which is completely dark, without any means of letting light in. Then someone knocks a hole in the wall and makes a window. The light is let in and the room illuminated. But we can also now see the outside world through the window – a world which was always there but which we couldn't see properly before. Jesus is a window into God; he is the light of God who has come into the world to illuminate it, and who lets us see God. Perhaps the window is not as large as we would like and perhaps the glass is less clear than we would like (1 Corinthians 13:12 is worth noting here), but God is suddenly made available for us in a new way. Many of us know what it is like to get up early in the morning, stepping out of bed into a dark room – when we open the curtains, the room is suddenly flooded with light and the outside world beckons to us. The same sense of excitement, like a dark room being flooded with light, or a beautiful landscape opening up before our eyes, can perhaps be felt when reading the prologue to the fourth gospel (John 1:1–18).

The second piece of glass is a mirror. As we look in a mirror, we see ourselves reflected. As we look at Christ, we see ourselves reflected as we shall finally be – man in a perfect relationship with God. Jesus discloses to us what it is like to be truly human, to live with God and for God. As we look at him, we are made painfully aware of just how far we have to go before we're anything like him! But the vision of restored and redeemed humanity presented to us in Jesus Christ gives us a foretaste of the New Jerusalem, an encouragement as we try to grow more like him and a challenge to our commitment to the gospel which alone can transform us in this way. Two pieces of glass; two aspects of Jesus Christ.

All too often, critics of the incarnation dismiss the idea because it seems inconsistent with their understanding of God. These critics, however, seem to know *exactly* what God is like, and on the basis of this idea of God, reject the incarnation. But on what basis do they establish this idea of God? What source of knowledge do they possess which is denied to everyone else, and which is more reliable than the knowledge of God to be had in Jesus Christ? All too often, criticisms of the incarnation boil down to the simple, and not very significant, statement that someone somewhere has an idea of God which is inconsistent with the idea of the incarnation. But so what? Unless he can prove, beyond all reasonable doubt, that God is *really* like that, his criticism is not important. And the simple fact is that mankind has been unable to reach much in the way of agreement on what God is like. For the Christian, God is to be known and seen most reliably as we encounter him in Jesus Christ. That is the Christian view of God. It may be inconsistent with somebody else's view of God – but that doesn't entitle them to say that the Christian view of God, expressed in the incarnation, is *wrong*. All statements about God are ultimately a matter of faith (even those of the atheist), and the most that this critic can do is register his *disagreement* with the Christian viewpoint. To do more is to go far beyond the limited evidence available at his disposal.

Man has tried to think about the nature of God for some considerable time, without reaching much agreement. A philosopher in the classical theist tradition would regard the word 'God' as referring to some supreme absolute, about which man could say little. It was against this idea of God that the French philosopher Pascal protested when he wrote his famous words: 'The God of Abraham, Isaac and Jacob, not of the philosophers.' The deist would regard God as a heavenly watchmaker who, having wound up the universe and set it going, left it to its own devices. A Hindu would feel able to say, without the slightest sense of impropriety, 'I am God' – meaning that the one unchanging reality is spread among all existing things to such an extent that it can't be separated from any of them. The atheist would treat the word 'God' as referring to a distant supernatural ruler (who doesn't exist anyway) who hurls down arbitrary dictates to mankind from his Olympus, and imprisons man's spirit in time and space. And so on. We could give an exhaustive list of the various ideas about God which man has toyed around with since he began to think, but there would be little point in doing so. All that we want to make clear is that the word 'God' can mean any number of things. In countries within which Christianity has been dominant, of course, this difficulty may be less important than we have suggested, due to the influence of Christianity. But it obviously raises the question: what God are we actually talking about? How do we know what 'God' is like? Where can we find out?

All sorts of answers have, of course, been given to questions like these. God may be seen in a glorious sunset, in the night sky, in the ordering of the universe, to name but three answers to one of them ('Where can we see God?'). But the Christian insists that God is to be most reliably and completely known as he is revealed in the person of Jesus Christ. This is not to say that God may not be known, in various ways and to various degrees, by other means – it is simply to say that Christians believe that Jesus Christ is the closest encounter with God to be had in this life. God makes himself available for our acceptance or rejection in the figure of Jesus Christ. To have encountered Jesus is to have encountered God. St Paul refers to Jesus as the 'image of the invisible God' (Colossians 1:15). In the letter to the Hebrews, we find Jesus described as the 'stamp' of God's nature (Hebrews 1:3) – the Greek word used could refer to an image stamped upon a coin, conveying the idea of an exact likeness. The God with whom we are dealing is the 'God and Father of our Lord Jesus Christ' (1 Peter 1:3), the God who seeks us, finds us and meets us in Jesus Christ.

What sorts of things does the incarnation tell us about the 'God and Father of our Lord Jesus Christ'? Perhaps most obviously, it tells us that the God with whom we are dealing is no distant ruler who remains aloof from the affairs of his creatures, but one who is passionately concerned with them to the extent that he takes the initiative in coming to them. God doesn't just reveal things *about* himself – he reveals *himself* in Jesus Christ. Revelation is personal. It is not given in a set of propositions, a list of statements which we are meant to accept, but in a person. It is to Christ, and not to the creed, that the world must look for redemption. The creed points away from itself to the one hope of redemption, to Jesus Christ. It is not the creed but the astonishing act of God in history to which it bears witness which is the source of the saving power underlying the Christian proclamation. Christianity has always insisted that man can *know* – not just *know about* – God. God does not encounter us as an *idea*, but as a *person*. We may know much *about* the President of the United States, or the British Royal Family – but that doesn't mean that we *know* them. For someone to be *known* means that they want to *be known* – there must be a willingness on their part to let us know them. But God goes further than this. He takes the initiative in approaching us, in disclosing to us that he wants us to know him. God reveals himself to man, and by revealing himself, discloses his love for man and his desire to enter into a relationship with him. Just as the waiting father encountered the returning prodigal son, so God encounters us.

The incarnation speaks to us of a God who *acts* to demonstrate his love for us. That 'God is love' (1 John 4:8) is a deep and important truth – but far more important is the truth that God *acted* to demonstrate this love. 'In this the love of God was made manifest among us, that God sent his only Son into the world, so that we might live through him' (1 John 4:9). Actions, as we are continually reminded, speak louder than words. That 'God is love' could be misunderstood as a static timeless universal truth; that 'God so loved the world that he gave his only Son, that whoever believes in him should not perish but have eternal life' (John 3:16) makes it clear that God is dynamic, a living God, who acted in order to reveal the full extent of his love for us.

The incarnation speaks to us of God humbling himself in order to make himself known to us, to call us back to him, to reveal the full extent of his love towards us. The words of Emily Elliott are memorable:

> Thou didst leave thy throne and thy kingly crown
> When thou camest to earth for me.

Christianity does not teach that man has to climb a ladder into heaven in order to find God and be with him – rather, it teaches that God has come down that ladder in order to meet us and take us back with him. We don't have to become like God before we can encounter him, because God became *like us* first. God meets us right where we are, without preconditions. A very famous saying of Athanasius is worth noting here: 'God became man so that we might become God.' By this, he simply meant that God became man in order that man might enter into a relationship and fellowship with him. The personal relationship which Christians presently enjoy with God through Christ is a foretaste of the fuller and deeper fellowship we will one day enjoy.

The theme of the humility of God is expounded with great feeling in a famous passage, usually thought to be a Christian hymn going back even before the writings of Paul, which Paul quotes in much the same way as I have been quoting from hymns in this chapter:

> Though [Jesus Christ] was in the form of God, [he] did not count
> equality with God a thing to be grasped, but emptied himself,

taking the form of a servant, being born in the likeness of men. And being found in human form he humbled himself and became obedient unto death, even death on a cross (Philippians 2:6–8).

This passage brings to mind a vast range of images of great men humbling themselves in order to bring about something worthwhile. God stoops down in order to meet us where we are. We all know the story of the ancient king who chose to leave his life of luxury in his palace and live as a peasant among his people, in order to understand them and thus rule them better on his return.

A similar thought is expressed by Mrs Cecil F. Alexander in her famous Christmas carol:

> He came down from earth to heaven,
> Who is God and Lord of all,
> And his shelter was a stable,
> And his cradle was a stall:
> With the poor and mean and lowly
> Lived on earth our Saviour holy.

God himself enters into the world, the vale of soul-making, full of darkness and tragedy. It is this 'far country' into which the Father enters to call his lost children home. Let us remind ourselves of that celebrated statement of St John: 'The Word became flesh and dwelt among us' (John 1:14). The word translated by 'dwelt' could be translated more accurately as 'pitched his tent'. This translation presents us with a powerful image, undiminished by the passage of time. The image is that of a wandering people who dwell in tents (as Israel once did in the period looked back to by the prophets as a time when she was close to God). One day they awake to find a new tent pitched in their midst – God himself has come to dwell among them as they wander. God is with them.

'God is with us.' This great theme of the incarnation is summed up in the name *Emmanuel* (Matthew 1:20–23). We must appreciate the importance of names for the biblical writers. Not only does a name disclose something of the personality of the individual, but being allowed to give someone a name establishes your authority over them. In the creation accounts, it is man who is allowed to name the animals (Genesis 2:19–20) and thus to establish his authority over them. But man is not allowed to name God – it is God who reveals his name to man (Exodus 3:13–15). Man is not allowed to establish authority over God. So it is with Jesus. Mary and Joseph are told what the name of their child shall be – they didn't choose it themselves: 'You shall call his name Jesus, for he will save his people from their sins' (Matthew 1:21). The name 'Jesus' literally means 'God saves', just as 'Emmanuel' means 'God with us' (Matthew 1:23). What, then, does 'God being with us' mean? Two main meanings may be identified. First, God is on our side; secondly, God is present with us. We will look at these now.

'If God is for us, who is against us?' (Romans 8:31–32). 'God is with us' means 'God is on our side'. The birth of the Son of God demonstrates and proclaims that God is on our side, that he has committed himself to the cause of the salvation of sinful mankind. In the birth of the long-promised Saviour, in his death on the cross of Calvary and in his resurrection from the dead we have a demonstration, a proof, a guarantee that God stands by us. Christmas tells us that the God we are dealing with, the God and Father of our Lord Jesus Christ, is not a God who is indifferent to our fate but one who is passionately committed to our salvation, to redeeming us from sin and to raising us to eternal life on the last day.

Secondly, 'God is with us' means that God is present among us. We are not talking of a God who stands far off from his world, aloof and distant from its problems. We are dealing with a God who has entered into our human situation, who became man and dwelt among us as one of us – who knows *at first hand* what it is like to be frail, mortal and human, to suffer and to die. We cannot explain suffering, but we can say that God took it upon himself to follow this way. God became the man of suffering, so that he could enter into the mystery of death and resurrection. God knows what it is like to be human – an astonishing and comforting thought. We are not talking about God becoming *like* man, just as if he was putting on some sort of disguise so that he could be passed off as a man – we are talking about the God who created the world entering into that same world *as* man and *on man's behalf* in order to redeem him. God has not sent a messenger or a representative to help the poor creatures that we are – he has involved himself directly, redeeming his own creation, instead of getting someone else to do it for him. God is not like a general who issues orders to his troops from the safety of a bomb-proof shelter, miles away from the front line, but one who leads his troops from the front, having previously done all that he asks them to do in turn.

The suffering and pain of the world simply will not go away, and we have every right to dismiss those who tell us that one day all will be well – after we have adopted their particular solution to the world's ills. Realism now demands that we work towards the alleviation of misery and suffering, recognizing that the vision of its total elimination is utopian. The idea of a political revolution which will eliminate human misery and suffering has lost what little credibility it once had, and has probably caused just as much misery where it has become a dogma. What, then, may one say about God and suffering? Can anything be said which is of comfort? In the history of the world, four answers have been given. First, suffering is real and will not go away, but death comes as the end, and in death there is an end of suffering and eventual peace. Secondly, suffering is an illusion. It simply is not there, but is imagined. Thirdly, suffering is real, but we ought to be able to rise above it and recognize that it is of little importance. The Christian has the fourth answer: God suffered in Christ.

God knows what it is like to suffer. The letter to the Hebrews talks about Jesus being our sympathetic high priest (Hebrews 4:15) – someone who suffers along with us (which is the literal meaning of both the Greek word 'sympathetic' and the Latin word 'compassionate'). This thought does not explain suffering, although it may make it more tolerable to bear. For it is expressing the deep insight that God himself suffered at first hand as we suffer. We are given a new perspective on life. Christianity has always held that it is the suffering of Christ upon the cross which is the culmination, the climax, of his ministry. God shares in the darkest moments of his people.

There is a famous saying about the medical profession worth remembering here: 'Only the wounded physician can heal.' Whether this is true or not is a matter for debate. But it does highlight the fact that we are able to relate better to someone who has shared our problem, who has already been through what we are going through now – and triumphed over it. As many already know from experience, it is often difficult to relate to someone who hasn't shared our problem. One way of getting round this is the idea of empathy. You empathize with the other person's problems and fears. Even though you haven't shared them – and may not even be able to understand them – you let them think that you have and that you understand exactly how they must be feeling. It works splendidly – provided the person you're trying to help doesn't see through it! The incarnation speaks of God *sympathizing* with our sufferings – not *empathizing*, as if he himself hadn't experienced them at first hand. God sympathizes in the strict sense of suffering alongside with us. In turning to God, we turn to one who knows and understands.

There is a splendid story once told about shepherds in East Anglia, formerly the centre of England's wool trade. When a shepherd died, he would be buried in a coffin stuffed full of wool. The idea was that, when the day of judgement came, Christ would see the wool and realize that this man had been a shepherd. As he himself had once been a shepherd, he would know the pressures the man had faced, the amount of time needed to look after wayward sheep and would understand why he hadn't been to church much! The story does, however, make an important point which we must treasure as one of the greatest of the many Christian insights into God. We are not dealing with a distant God who knows nothing of what being human, frail and mortal means. He knows and understands, and so we can 'with confidence draw near to the throne of grace' (Hebrews 4:16).

*   *   *   *

Who was Jesus? In this part of the book, we have been looking at questions about the *identity* of Jesus. But Christianity has much to say about the *significance* of Jesus – about what he *did*. In this part, we have been looking mainly at the birth and resurrection of Jesus Christ. In the next part, our attention moves to the cross. Why did Jesus have to die? And what are the implications for us, living some two thousand years after that event? Why is the cross universally recognized as the symbol of the Christian faith? Let us now move on to deal with questions like these.

PART 3
The Work of Jesus Christ

8

The New Testament Witness to the Work of Jesus

As I have emphasized throughout this book, Christianity is not the religion taught or preached by Jesus. It centres on the great drama of redemption accomplished by his death and resurrection. Nor is it primarily concerned with the life of a holy man or hero who serves as an example to his followers, but with a series of events in history which are recognized as acts of divine redemption. From the time of the New Testament onwards, the Christian church has always proclaimed the necessity, the possibility and the actuality of redemption through the death of Christ. Thus the New Testament witness to the identity and significance of Jesus Christ culminates in his death and resurrection, rather than in his moral teaching. This is most evident in the New Testament letters, although, as we saw earlier, the same concentration on his death and resurrection may be seen as underlying the gospels as well. It is evident from the New Testament that Jesus' death was not seen as an accident, the untimely or premature end to the career of a promising rabbi, but something through which God was working to achieve some definite purpose.

At some point, however, we have to turn from facts to interpretations of their significance. The death and resurrection of Jesus may, as we have insisted, be regarded as historical events. But what do they *mean*? Why are they significant? We have already emphasized the important distinction between an event and its interpretation: there is all the difference in the world between the statements 'Jesus died' and 'Jesus died for me'. The former refers to an event, the latter to its interpretation. In this part of the work, we are going to look at *interpretations* of the significance of the death and resurrection of Jesus Christ. These are sometimes called 'theories of the atonement' (although this phrase is not particularly helpful or illuminating). The previous part dealt with the question of the *person* of Christ; we are now concerned with the *work* of Christ.

The New Testament uses a wide range of images to express the richness of its understanding of the work of Christ. We may describe these images as analogies, models or metaphors – but the important point to appreciate is that we are attempting to explain or interpret what was going on between God, man and Christ in the crucifixion and resurrection in terms of ideas we are already familiar with from everyday life. The New Testament writers did exactly what every good preacher is meant to do – use illustrations and analogies drawn from their experience to help 'unpack' their theology. What happened on the cross cannot be reduced to a single statement or image. We have to build up a picture of what was going on by using a wide range of illustrations, each of which casts light on one particular aspect of our subject. It may well be that one individual finds one illustration more helpful than another – but this does not entitle him to argue that it is this illustration, and this illustration alone, which is good enough to stand on its own as a description of what was going on. Let us begin by looking at seven images the New Testament uses to bring out the meaning of the death and resurrection of Jesus Christ.

1. Ransom

The idea of Jesus giving his life as a ransom is found on the lips of Jesus himself in the Synoptic Gospels. Jesus came 'to give his life as a ransom for many' (Mark 10:45). If Jesus spoke Aramaic – which seems highly likely – it is possible that we could translate this as 'give his life as a ransom for *all*', because it is impossible to distinguish between 'many' and 'all' in Aramaic. The idea is also found elsewhere. 1 Timothy 2:5–6 is particularly important: 'For there is one God, and there is one mediator between God and men, the man Christ Jesus, who gave himself as a ransom for all.' A ransom is, of course, a price which is paid to achieve someone's freedom. In the Old Testament, however, it is evident that the emphasis falls upon the idea of being freed, of liberation, rather than speculation about the nature of the price paid, or about the identity of the person to whom it is paid. Thus Isaiah 35:10 and 51:11 refer to the liberated Israelites as the 'ransomed of the Lord'. The basic idea is that God intervenes to deliver his people from captivity, whether from the power of Babylon (Isaiah 51:10–11) or death (Hosea 13:14).

The early fathers were intrigued by the question of to whom the ransom was paid. Some developed the idea that Christ's death was a ransom paid to the devil, so that the satanic dominion over man might be broken and man might be freed. However, as we all know only too well from experience, analogies break down very quickly! The important thing to remember when dealing with an analogy is that the crucial point which the analogy illustrates must be identified. A similar point applies to metaphors. For example, an enthusiastic gardener might survey his magnificent display of blooming half-hardy annuals swaying in the wind, and refer to them as a 'sea of colour'. By that, he means that the observer is confronted with a vast expanse of moving colour, similar to the impression created by the sea. He does not mean that they are wet or salty! The point which he is trying to make by the analogy must be identified and appreciated. To ask: 'To whom is the ransom of Jesus' life paid?' is rather like asking: 'Are the half-hardy annuals salty and wet?' We have failed to appreciate the point which is being made, and have concentrated our attention on something we weren't meant to think about at all. For the New Testament, 'ransom' means 'freedom' – and beyond this point the analogy breaks down. Fortunately, however, we have other analogies which we can use to explore the meaning of Christ's death. Let us go on to another rather similar to the one we've just been looking at.

2. Redemption

The basic idea expressed here is that of 'buying back'. An example all too familiar from English life in the nineteenth and early twentieth century is provided by the pawnbroker. After pawning an item, it is necessary to redeem it – to buy it back from the pawnbroker – to re-establish possession of the item. A similar idea underlies the practice of redeeming slaves, a familiar event in New Testament times. A slave could redeem himself by buying his freedom. The word used to describe this event could literally be translated as 'being taken out of the forum [the slave market]'. As with the idea of ransom, we are dealing with the notion of restoring someone to a state of liberty, with the emphasis laid upon liberation rather than upon the means used to achieve it. It is thus interesting to notice how the words 'redeemed' and 'ransomed' are used side by side at points in the Old Testament, for example, Isaiah 55:10–11; Jeremiah 31:11; Hosea 13:14 (RSV).

In the Old Testament, God is often said to redeem his people (Deuteronomy 7:8; 2 Samuel 7:23; Hosea 7:13; Zechariah 10:8). Once more, it is necessary to note that the emphasis falls upon the act of divine deliverance or liberation, rather than upon any money used to achieve this liberation (Isaiah 52:3 even makes it clear that money is not involved). The New Testament can use the term in the sense of being liberated from bondage – for example, bondage to the law (Galatians 3:13; 4:5). More often, however, the word is used in the more general sense of simply being set free (Revelation 5:9; 14:3–4). Here, as with the image of ransom, we are dealing with the idea of Christ's death and resurrection setting man free from his bondage to sin and death. Paul's repeated emphasis that Christians are slaves who have been 'bought with a price' (1 Corinthians 6:20; 7:23) does, however, remind us that we cannot overlook the fact that our present liberty is somehow related to the death of Christ.

3. Justification

The idea of justification – which became especially important within the church at the time of the Reformation in the sixteenth century – is used frequently by Paul. 'We are justified by faith' (Romans 5:1), and thus have peace with God. The notion of justification is based upon the idea of being 'put right', rather than being 'made righteous' or 'declared righteous'. Perhaps the English word 'rectification' expresses its meaning better. Man is put right with God, rather than being made morally righteous. Justification is about 'rightness' rather than 'righteousness'. When Paul speaks of 'justification by faith', he is expressing the idea that man becomes right with God through faith. It may be that Paul is saying that it is faith itself which puts man right with God, or that it is through faith that man receives something which puts him right with God, or that faith *is* the right relationship to God. This isn't actually terribly important for our purposes. The important thing is that man is understood to be placed in a right relationship with God through the death and resurrection of Christ (Romans 4:24–25).

There are two possible ways of drawing out the meaning of the word 'justification'. In the Old Testament, the idea often has forensic overtones – in other words, it can refer to legal proceedings. If an accused man is justified, he is declared to be in the right, or vindicated, by a judge in court. This idea can be transferred to the New Testament without difficulty. The idea that man is justified by the blood of Christ (Romans 5:9) may be understood to mean that a sinner is vindicated by God on account of the death of Christ.

A second way of approaching the concept of justification is to see it as referring to a personal relationship. Justification may then be understood as the establishment or re-establishment of a right relationship between God and man, in much the same way as a right relationship might be established or re-established between two people. 'Justification by faith' could be interpreted as meaning that faith *is* the right relationship between man and God. Genesis 15:6 is interpreted by some Old Testament scholars to mean that Abraham, by believing God, placed himself in a right relationship with him.

4. Salvation

This idea is used frequently in the New Testament (Acts 13:26; Ephesians 1:13; Hebrews 1:14). The way in which the idea is used in the New Testament (the verb is generally used in the future tense) suggests that it should be thought of as a future event – something which is still to happen, although it may have begun to happen in the present. The basic idea is that of deliverance, preservation or rescue from a dangerous situation. The verb is used outside the New Testament to refer to being saved from death by the intervention of a rescuer, or to being cured from a deadly illness. It can also refer to being kept in good health. The word 'salvation' is thus used by the Jewish historian Josephus to refer to the deliverance of the Israelites from Egyptian bondage.

Two ideas are thus suggested by the concept. The first idea is that of being rescued or delivered from a dangerous situation. Just as the Israelites were delivered from their captivity in Egypt at the time of the Exodus, so Christ is understood to deliver man from the fear of death and the power of sin. The name 'Jesus' means 'God saves', and it is clear that the New Testament means 'saves from sin' (Matthew 1:21 is interesting here).

The second idea is that of 'wholeness' or 'health'. There is a very close relation between the ideas of salvation and wholeness. In many languages, the words for 'health' and 'salvation' are one and the same. Thus it is sometimes difficult to know whether a passage should be translated in terms of salvation or wholeness – for example, should the Greek version of Mark 5:34 be translated as 'Your faith has made you whole' or 'Your faith has saved you'? This close association of ideas was also found in the English language until the time of the Norman Conquest in 1066. The Old English word for salvation *hoel* (note the similarity to the modern English words 'heal' and 'health') was replaced by the Latin form 'salvation' at that time, so that the English-speaking world has lost this close association of both words and concepts. But in other modern languages, this close association remains. Let us explore its meaning.

When someone who has been ill is healed, he is restored to his former state of health, of wholeness. The creation stories of Genesis make it clear that God created man in a state of wholeness and that this wholeness was lost through the Fall. Just as healing involves restoring man's health, so salvation involves restoring man's wholeness, restoring him to the state in which he was first created by God. Paul draws attention to the relation between the first and the second Adam (Christ): through Adam, man lost his integrity before God; through Christ, that integrity can be regained and restored. In many respects the gospel is like a medicine – something which heals us, even though we don't understand how it works. It doesn't matter that we do not fully understand exactly how God is able to work out our salvation through the death and resurrection of Christ. The point is that Christians have always believed that God could and did save man in this way, even if they couldn't quite understand how or why (although they were certainly prepared to speculate over these questions).

Let us develop this medical analogy a little further, to bring this point out. When I was very young I developed a bad infection which had to be treated with antibiotics. I took my penicillin, as directed by the doctor, and the infection cleared up. I hadn't the slightest idea what the drug was or how it worked – I just trusted the doctor's diagnosis and the cure he prescribed. Many years later, as an Oxford undergraduate studying biochemistry, I learned how penicillin actually worked, the way in which it destroyed bacteria. Yet, I remember thinking at the time, it worked perfectly well without my understanding exactly what was happening! In many ways there is an obvious parallel with the gospel proclamation of salvation in Christ which diagnoses our problem (sin) and offers us a cure (Christ). We don't know exactly how Christ overwhelms sin – although in this part of the book we'll be looking at some suggestions – but we firmly believe, on the best authority, that he *does*. The theologian may fuss over the details, but the crucial thing is our belief that Christ somehow provides a solution to the problem of the human situation.

'Your faith has made you whole' – by restoring man to fellowship with God, and beginning the long and painful process of learning to live with God and for God. Why should it be painful? Because for so long we have tried to live without God, when we finally come to adjust our lives to make room for him, we find it very difficult to make the adjustment. Many of us know only too well what happens when the blood circulation is cut off from an arm or leg. When the circulation is restored it is acutely painful as the limb tries to readjust to the presence of the live-giving fluid. Yet that pain comes about through the limb coming to life again. So it is with coming back to God. It is painful, but it is also coming back to life.

5. Reconciliation

'In Christ God was reconciling the world to himself' (2 Corinthians 5:19). This famous statement draws our attention to the idea of 'reconciliation'. The word and the idea are all too familiar to us all. The world in which we live cries out for reconciliation – reconciliation of employers and employees, of husband and wife, of parents and children. Paul uses the word in another context to refer to a reconciliation of an estranged husband and wife (1 Corinthians 7:11). The idea of reconciliation is fundamental to human experience, especially in the area of personal relationships. The parable of the prodigal son (Luke 15:11–32) is perhaps the supreme illustration of the importance of reconciliation in the New Testament. It illustrates vividly the reconciliation of father and son, and the restoration of their broken relationship.

The parallel between the reconciliation of two individuals and between man and God will be obvious. God is treated as a person, someone to whom man can relate. Their relationship, once close (as in Eden), has been seriously disrupted to the point where it exists in name only. Man is, and will always remain, a son of God – it is God who has created him and it is God who continues to love him, despite man's journey into the far country away from God. It must be emphasized that the prodigal son remained the son of his father even when he set off to live independently, confident that he could live without his father's continual presence and oversight. But that relationship exists in name only – one party to the relationship acts as if it was not there. Reconciliation takes place when both parties to a relationship take the relationship with full seriousness, and acknowledge their mutual love for each other and the obligations which they have towards each other. The son returns to his father and they embrace – the relationship becomes *real*.

Reconciliation involves someone taking the initiative. If there are two persons who once enjoyed a close relationship but now have drifted apart, that relationship will remain broken unless someone attempts a reconciliation. Someone – usually one of the two parties to the relationship – has to take the initiative and approach the other party, acknowledging that the relationship has gone wrong, recalling how precious and important that relationship once was, affirming their love and concern for the other and asking them to restore the relationship. If the other party is not prepared to restore the relationship, no progress has been made. If reconciliation is offered but not accepted, the relationship remains unaltered. There is simply no such thing as a 'legal fiction' in personal relationships. If, and only if, both parties agree to restore the relationship will reconciliation be achieved. All this is evident from our experience of the niceties of everyday personal relationships. By making an appeal to personal relationships – and the parable of the prodigal son makes this appeal with remarkable power – the New Testament grounds our relationship with God in everyday experience.

'In Christ God was reconciling the world to himself.' How is Christ understood to be involved in the reconciliation between man and God? There are two ways of looking at this question. First, the phrase 'In Christ God was' is taken as a reference to the incarnation. In other words, God incarnate makes his reconciling appeal to man. Christ, as God incarnate, takes the initiative in proclaiming the overwhelming love of God for man and the divine wish that man should be reconciled to him. In proclaiming the need and possibility of reconciliation to God, Christ addresses us as God and on behalf of God.

Secondly, the phrase 'in Christ' is understood to reflect a Hebrew grammatical construction with which Paul would have been familiar, which would be better translated as 'through Christ'. In other words, 'Through Christ God was reconciling the world to himself.' Christ is understood as the agent of divine reconciliation, the one through whom God reconciles us to him, the mediator or go-between. The following remarks from the letter to the Colossians are instructive: 'And you, who once were estranged and hostile in mind ... he has now reconciled in his body of flesh by his death' (Colossians 1:21–22). The ideas of 'estrangement' (or 'alienation', as it could also be translated) and 'hostility' are used to refer to man's initial relationship with God, which is transformed through the death of Christ into reconciliation.

A further idea associated with the reconciliation of God and man through the death of Christ is peace. Reconciliation means the end of hostility and the beginning of peace. Through Christ, God was pleased 'to reconcile to himself all things ... making peace by the blood of his cross' (Colossians 1:20). Here Christ is seen as a mediator between God and man, pleading God's case to man and man's case to God, abolishing the hostility between them and establishing a new relationship of peace and harmony. Christ makes an appeal to us on behalf of God that we should be reconciled to him. Paul continues his discussion of the reconciliation of man to God as follows: 'In Christ God was reconciling the world to himself, not counting their trespasses against them, and entrusting to us the message of reconciliation. So we are ambassadors for Christ, God making his appeal through us' (2 Corinthians 5:19–20). The idea here is that believers are representatives of Christ in the world, just as an embassy is the representative of a country or monarch in a foreign land.

The emphasis upon the divine initiative is important: it is *God* who reconciles us to him – not the other way round. God approaches us, and it is up to us to respond. It is God who takes upon himself the pain and the anguish of broaching the situation of human sin, attempting to let us know of the great distress which sin causes him and the barrier it places between him and us. 'Your sins have made a separation between you and your God,' in the famous words of the prophet (Isaiah 59:2). It is God who discloses to us the full extent of his love for us, despite the fact that we are sinners. Our love of God is a result of his love for us, not the other way round: 'In this is love, not that we loved God but that he loved us and sent his Son to be the expiation for our sins' (1 John 4:10).

6. Adoption

The image of adoption is used by Paul to express the distinction between sons of God (believers) and *the* Son of God (Jesus Christ). The most important passages are Romans 8:15, 23; 9:4; Galatians 4:5; Ephesians 1:5. It is clear that this is a legal image. A father would be free to adopt individuals from outside his natural family and give them a legal status of adoption, thus placing them within the family. Although a distinction would still be possible between the natural and adopted children, they have the same legal status – in the eyes of the law they are all members of the same family, irrespective of their origins.

Paul uses this image to indicate that, through faith, believers come to have the same status as Jesus (as sons of God), without implying that they had the same divine nature as Jesus. Faith brings about a change in man's status before God, incorporating him within the family of God, despite the fact that he does not share the same divine origins as Christ.

7. Forgiveness

This is perhaps the most powerful and familiar image used to explain the significance of Christ's death and resurrection. The image can be interpreted in two ways: as a *legal* concept and as a *personal* concept. The legal use of the term is probably most familiar from the parable of the merciless servant (Matthew 18:23–35). Here forgiveness is understood in terms of the remission of a debt. The servant is so heavily in debt to his master that he cannot pay it – and as an act of compassion, the master forgives him the debt. In other words, he writes it off, cancels it. The idea of 'forgiveness of sins' may thus be regarded as a legal concept, involving the remission of penalty.

The second sense of the term is probably more familiar, and is clearly closely related to the idea of reconciliation. Forgiveness is here understood as something necessary for a personal relationship to be restored to its former state after a hurtful disagreement or misunderstanding. Once more, it is necessary for one party – in this case, the offended party – to offer the other forgiveness. Once more, it is necessary for him to broach a difficult and painful situation in order to restore the relationship. If it is not accepted, the relationship remains unaltered. Forgiveness offered, yet not accepted, does not transform a relationship. As with the idea of reconciliation, we are presented with the concept of a personal, and greatly hurt, God offering to man his forgiveness.

We have now looked at seven analogies or illustrations of what Christ achieved on the cross. Perhaps it is worth noting that they broadly fall under three categories.

1. *The commercial or transactional approach.* Here Christ's death is understood as the basis of a transaction by means of which man is transferred from bondage to liberty. Obvious examples are the ideas of ransom and redemption.

2. *The legal approach.* Here Christ's death is understood as the means by which a change in man's legal status is achieved – for example, being vindicated of guilt, being adopted into a family, or being forgiven a debt.

3. *The personal approach.* Here Christ's death is understood as the means by which a personal relationship between God and man is restored – for example, being made 'right with God', reconciliation and forgiveness.

It would be possible to extend this list considerably and give an exhaustive list of ideas, analogies or metaphors used to explain what it was that Christ achieved on the cross. This exercise would probably be interesting, but is not particularly relevant to our purposes. In the following three chapters we propose to look at three main 'theories of the atonement' – ways of making sense of the significance of the death of Christ – which have been influential over the last two thousand years of Christian history. These theories are basically attempts to develop insights contained in the New Testament in a more systematic manner. We begin with the theory that Christ's death is a demonstration of the divine love, sometimes called the 'moral' or 'exemplarist' theory of the atonement.

9

The Loving God

The death of Jesus Christ demonstrates the overwhelming love of God for sinful man. Perhaps the most famous statement of the extent of this love may be found in John's gospel: 'God so loved the world that he gave his only Son, that whoever believes in him should not perish but have eternal life' (John 3:16). But how does the death of Christ demonstrate this love of God for man?

The theme of the love of God for his people is deeply embedded in both the Old and the New Testaments. One of the great themes expounded by the Old Testament prophets is the love of God for Israel which he demonstrated by delivering her from bondage in Egypt and leading her into the promised land. The eighth-century prophets in particular portray God reflecting with sadness on the way the child whom he loved so dearly has wandered away from him. One of the most powerful statements of this theme may be found in the prophet Hosea: 'When Israel was a child, I loved him, and out of Egypt I called my son. The more I called them, the more they went from me ... Yet it was I who taught Ephraim to walk, I took them up in my arms; but they did not know that I healed them. I led them with cords of compassion, with the bands of love' (Hosea 11:1–4). Israel is portrayed as the wayward child of God, whom God brought

137

into being, cared for and supported while still incapable of looking after herself, and finally led into the promised land. Just as a mother can never forget the child to whom she gave birth, so God can never forget his people (Isaiah 49:14–15). Even though Israel abandons and rejects her God, God continues to love her (Hosea 14:4). God is frequently portrayed as musing over the delight he will feel when Israel returns to him to dwell under his protection (Hosea 14:4–7). The great covenant formula – 'You will be my people, and I will be your God' – is seen as establishing a relationship between God and his people which nothing can destroy. It may be threatened by the great empires of the world, or by the disobedience of Israel herself, yet God, in his love, remains faithful to his people.

This theme is taken up and developed in the New Testament, perhaps most powerfully in the parable of the prodigal son (Luke 15:11–32). We all know this story far too well to need to tell it again here. The son goes off into the far country, only to realize his stupidity, and longs to return home to his father. Yet he is convinced that his father will have disowned him, will no longer wish to acknowledge him as his son. Every age has its own 'far country', and is thus able to identify with the parable with remarkable ease. But it is perhaps worth noting that the title traditionally given for the parable is not quite right. It is certainly true that the parable deals with a prodigal (the word means 'wasteful') son – but it also deals with a waiting father.

In this parable we see a reflection of the relationship between man and God. And the remarkable feature of the parable is the picture of God which it gives us. The father sees the returning son – he has been waiting – long before the son notices him, and rushes out to meet him. Although the parable indicates that the son had come to his senses and wanted to admit his stupidity to his father, he isn't given a chance to do this. The father embraced him before he could say a word, and made abundantly clear the full extent of his love for the son whom he thought he had lost.

The New Testament takes this idea of the overwhelming love of God for sinners a stage further by specifically linking it with the death of Christ. As Paul puts it: 'God shows his love for us in that while we were yet sinners Christ died for us' (Romans 5:8). In this passage, Paul reflects upon the sort of people we might feel prepared to die for. Perhaps we could think of some remarkable, outstanding person who is clearly so good that we would have no hesitation in giving our lives in order to save theirs (Romans 5:7) – but it might be difficult to think of someone like this. For Paul, this thought just brings home still further the immensity of the love of God for sinners. Even while we were still sinners – before we repented or improved ourselves – Christ died for us. In human terms, the greatest demonstration of love a human being can manage is also his last – he gives the greatest thing which he has, his own life. 'Greater love has no man than this, that a man lay down his life for his friends' (John 15:13).

Examples of this behaviour are quite rare in everyday life, and are all the more memorable when we encounter them. All too many date from the time of the First World War, with its previously unimagined horrors. The story is often told of a soldier in the trenches who saw his comrade fall wounded some distance from the safety of his own lines. Rather than leave him to die, he crawled the considerable distance to where the man lay, and brought him back. As he tried to lower his friend into the trench, he himself was hit by a sniper's bullet and mortally wounded. As he lay dying, he was told that his friend would live, and he was able to die with that knowledge. He had given his life for a friend. Doubtless many other – and even more pathetic – examples of this sort of behaviour could be given. It illustrates human love forced to its absolute limits, in that the man who gives his life for his friend does not even enjoy the satisfaction of his future company. All is given, and nothing received – except, perhaps, an all too brief satisfaction that something worthwhile has been achieved.

It is clear that the New Testament writers regarded Christ as giving his life for a purpose. Equally, there can be no doubt that they understand it to represent a most powerful demonstration of the love of God for his people. But it is also far more than that, and implies far more than meets the eye. In the last two centuries there has been a grow-ing tendency in some quarters to insist that the death of Christ is a demonstration of the love of God for us – and nothing more than that. The image of Christ loving, suffer-ing and finally dying evokes a deep response in man, causing him to love God in return – and nothing more. There is no need to involve the idea of an incarnation of God, the resurrection, original sin, or vicarious suffering – simply the idea of love begetting love. What traditionally had been seen as one aspect of a greater whole is treated as if it were all that could be said about the meaning of the death of Christ. It is this theory which is sometimes referred to as the 'moral' or 'exemplarist' theory of the atonement, and has achieved some popularity in the more rationalist sections of the Christian church. There are, however, cer-tain serious difficulties which must be noted in connection with it.

First, we must ask exactly how we know that the death of Christ represents a demonstration of the love *of God* for man. For traditional Christian belief there is no difficulty about this whatsoever. Christ is God incarnate, and in the image of the dying Christ we see God himself giving himself up for his people. The great hymn of Charles Wesley exults in this thought:

> Amazing love! how can it be
> That thou, my God, shouldst die for me?

The great paradox of the immortal God giving himself up to death on behalf of the people whom he loves is nothing less than amazing, and is the theme of much reflection within the Christian tradition. To return to Wesley:

> 'Tis mystery all! The Immortal dies:
> Who can explore His strange design?
> In vain the first-born seraph tries
> To sound the depths of love divine!

By giving himself up to death, the incarnate God demonstrated the full depths of his love for mankind. It is indeed the love *of God* which we are dealing with, in that it is none other than God himself who loved us and gave himself for us.

But is it actually possible to get rid of the idea of Christ being God incarnate, as many of those inclined towards rationalism think? Christ is now seen as a man – a very special man, to be sure – but a man none the less. Christ is therefore to be thought of as making the greatest sacrifice which man can make – giving his life for others. But is this the love *of God*? Clearly it is not. It represents the height of human love – what the love of God might well be *like*. But in that Christ is not God incarnate, it is not the love of God which we are dealing with. If Christ is not God in any meaningful sense of the word, the best we can look for is information about what the love of God is (or might be) like – and not a demonstration of what the love of God actually is. A messenger or delegate can tell us that – but only God himself can show us. The soldier we mentioned above demonstrated exactly this love in giving his life for his friend – and we would not dream of suggesting that this was the love of God.

Why are we justified in singling out Christ as the supreme demonstration of the love of God? For the traditional

Christian, the answer is evident: Christ is God incarnate, and thus commands our attention for that very reason. But if he is not God incarnate, we must justify his uniqueness in some other way. This actually proves to be remarkably difficult. Outstanding human acts of love are certainly rare – but in the course of human history, so many such acts have taken place that the best we could manage is to identify Jesus as one among many. And is there not some truth in the suggestion that the idea of the uniqueness of Christ is actually a doctrine of traditional Christianity, based upon the idea of the incarnation, which rationalism has inherited and tried to reinterpret in terms which would not establish that uniqueness in the first place? In other words, the traditional Christian ideas about Christ are retained by rationalists, yet reinterpreted in such a way that they lose their force (even if they become more credible to the sceptical mind)?

Let us take this point a little further. There are certainly those who would suggest that the idea of Jesus showing the love of God is a perfectly adequate statement of the gospel. But, in reply, we must make an historical point: this version of Christianity would hardly have survived in the world into which Christianity first exploded. It may be that this is a reinterpretation of the Christian understanding of what happened on the cross which makes sense to modern man – but it certainly would have cut no ice in the past. It is difficult to see why this idea should catch the imagination of man. Man has always shown himself remarkably ungrateful for even the most interesting pieces of information – and that is all we are dealing with in this view of the death of Christ: the information that God loves us. But so what? After all, why should Christ's sufferings be regarded as such overwhelming demonstrations of divine love? Unless mankind was involved in some terrible predicament, and unless Christ's death could be shown to be directly related to that predicament, it is difficult to see why man should be even remotely interested in, or grateful to, Jesus. And once we start talking about 'man's predicament', we are moving on to rather different understandings of the significance of the death of Christ!

The 'moral' or 'exemplarist' theory of the atonement seems to presuppose that man's basic problem is that of ignorance – he doesn't know what God is really like. Thus he may think that God doesn't love him. The death of Jesus on the cross educates him – it informs him that God really does love him. The theory appeals to those inclined to rationalism because it seems to eliminate ideas which they find difficult, such as the incarnation, resurrection, or human bondage to sin. But it just isn't that simple. Let us ask some reasonable questions. Is it *really* the love of God which is revealed? A more credible interpretation is that it is a splendid example of *human* love – man's love for man – which is revealed. And what point did it serve? None – except possibly Barabbas – can be said to have benefitted directly from his death. The idea of Jesus dying to make some sort of theological point also strains the imagination somewhat. Why did God reveal that he loved man in such a strange way? Why did it take the death of Jesus to prove this? Why couldn't God just have told us that he loved us, instead of going about conveying exactly the same information in such a complicated and ambiguous way? Ambiguous? Yes – because it is far from clear what information, if anything, is being revealed about God.

Let us develop this point about the ambiguity of the cross. Traditional Christianity has always insisted that the cross represents, among other things, the disclosure of the full extent of God's love for sinful mankind. Working on the basis of a theology of the incarnation – in other words, the belief that it is God incarnate who is himself dying on the cross – this idea makes perfect sense. But if the theology of the incarnation is discarded in order to make way for a simpler view of the death of Christ, what are we left with? What reasons do rationalists have for suggesting that it is the love of God which is being revealed? Why can rationalists reject the idea that the death of Christ shows that God is totally uninvolved in his world? Why can rationalists reject the idea that the cross is completely meaningless? Why can rationalists reject the idea that the cross reveals the terrible wrath of God? Why can rationalists reject the idea that the terrible death of a wonderful man like Jesus shows that God is an arbitrary tyrant who enjoys inflicting suffering on the innocent? In short – why can rationalists reject all these ideas in favour of the idea that the cross reveals the love of God? It is not the most obvious of explanations. It is far from clear what, if anything, this theory tells us about God. The answer would seem to be that traditional Christianity has, on the basis of its understanding of the incarnation and resurrection, rightly insisted that the cross reveals the love of God – and this idea has been taken over by rationalism, although the theological framework which gave and guaranteed this explanation is discarded. If this is so, we are entitled to make an important observation: this theory of the atonement is ultimately dependent upon a theology of the incarnation and resurrection, and logical consistency demands that this be recognized. In other words, this rationalist theory of the atonement is actually much more complicated than might at first be thought.

A further point we might consider is the following: God can be left out of this theory with the greatest of ease, and apparently without making much difference. As we have seen, if Jesus is not God incarnate, we are not talking about a revelation of the love of *God* but the love of *man*. And if Jesus shows us the limits of man's love for man, and inspires us to imitate his example, why do we need to bring God into the theory? It works perfectly well without him. It is simply

moralism, providing us with information about the way in which we ought to behave, rather than with reliable information about God. Christ is treated as a moral example, showing man what he is capable of. In other words, Jesus is an example of what every man could be. He is different in degree, and not in kind, from the rest of mankind. But why, then, is Jesus special? Mankind has been fortunate enough to have lots of splendid moral and religious teachers in the course of history, showing in their lives the principles which they taught. Why should Jesus be special?

The traditional answer to this question is perfectly straightforward: the resurrection demonstrates Jesus' identity as the Son of God, expressed in the idea of the incarnation. Jesus is special because of his unique relationship to God. If this view of the identity and significance of Jesus is abandoned, the special place which Christians give Jesus will have to be justified on some other grounds. But what grounds might these be? The excellence of his moral teaching? But Christians have tended to treat Jesus' teaching with great respect on account of who they knew he was, rather than working out who he was on the basis of what he taught. And Christians simply do not follow Jesus as you might follow Socrates or Gandhi (people whose lives and views do indeed deserve to be respected) in the way this theory suggests. Once more, we see that this theory of the atonement is simply derivative or parasitic – it actually depends upon insights drawn from the framework of traditional Christianity which rationalism prefers to discard. Whether they can actually do this is open to serious question.

Finally, it must be asked whether this theory of the atonement has a realistic view of man. Is man really capable of recognizing the death of Christ as a revelation of the love of God, and responding to it? What happens if man's will is so corrupted that he is incapable of making a response like this?

Tennyson's famous words in his great poem *In Memoriam* seem hopelessly idealistic:

> We needs must love the highest when we see it.

The more cynical observation of antiquity seems much closer to our experience: we see the good and approve of it – but we actually go and do something worse.

Earlier, we noticed how Christians worshipped and adored Jesus as their Saviour and Lord, praying to him and praising him as if he were God himself. The view of Jesus expressed in the 'moral' or 'exemplarist' theory of the atonement doesn't fit in with this at all. It is certainly true that the death of Christ demonstrates the love of God for man – nobody is going to deny that. But this love of God is grounded in the idea of the one who was rich beyond all splendour, becoming poor for our sake. As the Nicene Creed puts it: 'For us men, and for our salvation, he came down from heaven.' We might go back to Charles Wesley's famous hymn:

> He left His Father's throne above,
> So free, so infinite His grace;
> Emptied Himself of all but love,
> And bled for Adam's helpless race.

The full wonder of the love of God for man can only be appreciated when we recognize what the incarnation and crucifixion really mean. God humbles himself and stoops down to meet man where he is. The first Christians believed, as we still believe, that Jesus was the embodiment of God, God incarnate, God giving himself to mankind. In the incarnation we see God giving his own self. At Calvary, God took upon himself the suffering, the pain and the agony of the world. God showed the full extent of his love by coming and suffering himself – not by sending a messenger or a substitute. It helps to know that in the seemingly senseless

and pointless suffering of Jesus, God himself is present, sharing in the tragedies of the human race. Jesus did not come to explain away or to take away suffering – he came to take it upon himself, to assume human suffering and lend it dignity and meaning through his presence and sympathy. It is *this* which is the full-blooded meaning of the love of God, rather than the anaemic travesty of this idea to be found in the 'moral' theory of the atonement.

In contemplating the appalling spectacle of Jesus dying on the cross, we come to see none other than God taking upon himself the agony of the world which he created and loves. It is *this* which is the 'love of God' in the full-blooded sense of the word. John Donne expresses this thought:

> Wilt thou love God, as he thee? then digest
> My soul, this wholesome meditation,
> How God the Spirit, by angels waited on
> In heaven, doth make his temple in thy breast.
> The Father having begot a Son most blessed,
> And still begetting (for he ne'er begun)
> Hath deigned to choose thee by adoption,
> Coheir to his glory, and Sabbath's endless rest;
> And as a robbed man, which by search doth find
> His stol'n stuff sold, must lose or buy it again:
> The Son of glory came down, and was slain,
> Us whom he had made, and Satan stol'n, to unbind.
> T'was much, that man was made like God before,
> But, that God should be made like man, much more.

In its deepest sense, the love of God for man is that of a God who stoops down from heaven to enter into the world of men, with all its agony and pain, culminating in the grim cross of Calvary.

We could extend the parable of the prodigal son to say that God himself went into the far country to meet us and bring us home. Earlier we noted the story from the time of the First World War of the soldier who went out into No Man's Land – the 'far country' – from the safety of his trench

in order to bring his beloved comrade home. He did – but it
cost him his life. We left out one part, the final part, of that
pathetic story. As the soldier lay dying, knowing that he
had saved his friend, he whispered, 'I brought him through.'
The Son of God went into the far country and brought us
through, brought us home, though it cost him his life. It is
this astonishing love of God which lies at the heart of the
gospel proclamation:

> Love so amazing, so divine,
> Demands my soul, my life, my all!

Why is this overwhelming love of God for man so important? Love gives meaning to life in that the person loved
becomes special to someone, assumes a *significance* which he
otherwise might not have had. There is every danger that
man will feel lost and overwhelmed in the immensity of the
world. What place does he have in it? Is he in any way
special? Christianity makes the astonishing assertion – which
it bases upon the life, death and resurrection of Jesus Christ
– that God is profoundly interested in us and concerned for
us, despite our apparent indifference to him. Furthermore,
God is understood to give the fullness of his loving attention
to each and every one, the totality of his own personal
interest. The experience of love is perhaps one of the deepest and most important that human existence knows. Let us
take two people, one of whom cares passionately for the
other, yet keeps quiet about it. Then the other finds out,
perhaps by chance, and realizes that he means something
special to someone else, that a new relationship is possible,
that at least in the eyes of one other person he is important
and precious. That moment of recognition can be devastating, and from that moment, life may be seen in a very
different light. So it is with God. The realization that we
mean something to God, that Christ died *for us*, that Christ
came to bring *us* back from the far country to our loving and
waiting father, means that we are special in the sight of God.

In the midst of an immense and frightening universe, we are given meaning and significance by the realization that the God who called the world into being, who created us, also loves us and cares for us, coming down from heaven and going to the cross to prove the full extent of that love to a disbelieving and wondering world.

10

The Victorious God

The theme of God's victory over hostile forces is often encountered in the Old Testament. Creation itself is frequently
regarded as a divine victory over the forces of chaos (Job
26:12–13; Psalms 89:9–10). This great theme of God's victory over sin, evil and oppression is, of course, most obvious
in the Old Testament accounts of the exodus from Egypt.
God is seen as having delivered his captive people from their
captivity, as having gained a great victory over the forces
of oppression and darkness. The great song of triumph in
Exodus 15 exults in this victory: 'I will sing to the Lord, for
he has triumphed gloriously; the horse and his rider he has
thrown into the sea. The Lord is my strength and my song,
and he has become my salvation' (Edoxus 15:1–2). It was
through this historic act of divine deliverance that Israel was
brought into existence as a people, and it is obvious that
Israel never forgot its importance. Time and time again the
Psalms recall that great act of divine victory and deliverance,
and look forward to similar divine victories in years to come
(Psalms 135 and 136 are worth reading at this point).

If the exodus from Egypt is viewed by the Old Testament
as a divine victory marking one turning point in the history of
Israel, the exodus from Babylon is viewed as the second. In
the sixth century before Christ, Jerusalem was besieged and
captured by the Babylonians, and many of the inhabitants of

Jerusalem deported to a life of exile in Babylon. It is this long period of exile which lies behind the deep sense of nostalgia found in Psalm 137: 'By the waters of Babylon, there we sat down and wept, when we remembered Zion. On the willows there we hung up our lyres. For there our captors required of us songs . . . saying, "Sing us one of the songs of Zion!" How shall we sing the Lord's song in a foreign land?' (Psalm 137:1–4). That captivity lasted half a century, and the exiles seem to have given up hope of ever seeing Jerusalem again. As that captivity wore on, a new prophet rose among the exiles, declaring that God would soon deliver his people from Babylon, just as he had once delivered them from Egypt (Isaiah 40–55). In a great moment of vision, the prophet sees God acting decisively to redeem his people:

> Awake, awake, put on strength, O arm of the Lord;
> Awake, as in days of old, the generations of long ago.
> Was it not thou that did cut Rahab in pieces, that didst pierce the dragon?
> Was it not thou that didst dry up the sea, the waters of the great deep;
> that didst make the depths of the sea a way for the redeemed to pass over?
> And the ransomed of the Lord shall return,
> and come to Zion with singing. (Isaiah 51:9–11).

The theme of the 'Lord [baring] his holy arm before the . . . nations' (Isaiah 52:10), which runs throughout this great prophecy, is a theme of divine victory and divine deliverance. It is this vision of the great and mighty acts of God in history, by which his people are delivered and preserved, which is summed up in one of the most famous passages in this prophecy:

> How beautiful upon the mountains are the feet of him who brings good tidings, who publishes peace, who brings good tidings of good, who publishes salvation, who says to Zion, 'Your god reigns.' Hark, your watchmen lift up their voice, together

they sing for joy; for eye to eye they see the return of the Lord to Zion. Break forth together into singing, you waste places of Jerusalem; for the Lord has comforted his people, he has redeemed Jerusalem (Isaiah 52:7–9).

This theme of the victory of God in delivering his people from captivity became deeply embedded in the hopes and expectations of Israel as the centuries passed. Israel once more came to be under foreign rule, first by the Greeks, then by the Romans. But the great theme of deliverance continued to be celebrated in the feast of the Passover.

The feast of the Passover celebrated – as it still celebrates today – the events leading up to the exodus and the establishment of the people of Israel. The passover lamb, slaughtered shortly before, and eaten at the feast, symbolizes this great act of divine redemption. It is thus very significant that the Last Supper and the crucifixion of Jesus took place at the feast of the Passover. The Synoptic Gospels clearly treat the Last Supper as a Passover meal, with Jesus initiating a new version of this meal. While Jews celebrated their deliverance by God from Egypt by eating a lamb, Christians would henceforth celebrate their deliverance by God from sin by eating bread and drinking wine. Passover celebrates the great act of God by which the people of Israel came into being; the eucharist celebrates the great act of God by which the Christian church came into being.

John's gospel seems to work with a slightly different date: Jesus is crucified at exactly the same moment as the slaughter of the passover lambs begins. It is not quite clear if or how the differences between the Synoptic and Johannine accounts can be resolved. But what is important here is the point which John's gospel wants to make: the *real* passover lamb is not being slaughtered in the temple precincts, but on the cross – 'Behold the Lamb of God, who takes away the sin of the world!' (John 1:29).

The very timing of the Last Supper and the crucifixion, and the close parallels with the Passover feast, make it clear

that the gospel writers see a close connection between the
exodus and the death of Christ. Both are to be seen as acts of
divine deliverance. Both are to be seen as acts of divine
victory. But it is in the New Testament letters, especially
those of Paul, that this idea is fully developed. Here, the
death and resurrection of Christ are often reaffirmed as a
decisive act of divine deliverance by which man has been
liberated from the tyranny of sin and death. Paul draws on
images of conflict taken from the battlefield, the amphi-
theatre and the athletic stadium to bring out the full significance of this theme of victory. 'Thanks be to God, who gives
us the victory through our Lord Jesus Christ' (1 Corinthians
15:57). For the writers of the New Testament, the forces of
evil are as real as the forces of good. Despite the fact that
they have little to say to explain its origins, they never
attempt to explain it away. For Paul, God 'disarmed the
principalities and powers and made a public example of
them, triumphing over them in him [Christ]' (Colossians
2:15). In John's gospel, we also find the cross interpreted as a
symbol of victory – victory over darkness, death and the
world (John 12:31–33 is particularly interesting). Thus the
final words of Jesus from the cross – 'It is finished' (John
19:30) – should not be seen as a cry of hopeless defeat – 'It is
all over' – but as a shout of triumph – 'It is accomplished!'
What had to be done, had been done, and done well.

The idea of God's victory over the forces of sin, death and
evil in the cross has always had enormous dramatic power,
making a strong appeal to man's imagination. The New
Testament writers are content to indicate that, somehow,
God achieved a great victory through the death of Christ and
that this victory affects believers here and now. But Christianity soon exploded into the first-century Mediterranean
world, and Christian preachers found that this way of looking at the death of Christ seemed to lack something – it
didn't explain why Christ had to die, for example. And so
they developed the idea along lines somewhat different to

those found in the New Testament. An illustration from the works of Gregory the Great, writing in the sixth century, will make this clear.

According to Gregory, the devil had managed to gain rights over man on account of man's sin, and God was not in a position to violate those rights in order to deliver man from the power of the devil. Therefore God devised a cunning plan by which the devil might be trapped. God sent into the world someone who looked like sinful man but who was actually sinless – in other words, Jesus Christ. The devil, not realizing that Jesus was sinless, naturally assumed that he could claim his rights over him, and eventually took his life. Gregory likens what happened next to a great fish being caught on a baited fish-hook. The devil saw only the bait (Christ's humanity) and not the hook (Christ's divinity), and so found himself trapped. Having overstepped his authority, the devil's rights over man were forfeited, and God was thus able to deliver man from the power of the devil. Other writers suggested that the cross was more like a mouse-trap than a fish-hook, but the same basic ideas were still used. It need hardly be added that the New Testament was quite innocent of this type of speculation!

Another way of approaching the New Testament's emphasis upon victory over sin and death through Christ may be found in a famous eleventh-century Easter hymn by Fulbert, Bishop of Chartres:

> For Judah's Lion burst his chains
> Crushing the serpent's head;
> And cries aloud through death's domain,
> To wake the imprisoned dead.

This highly imaginative hymn takes up the image of Jesus Christ as the conquering lion of the tribe of Judah, developed in the Book of Revelation (Revelation 5:5), who fulfils the great promise of redemption made to Adam that he will trample the serpent under his feet (Genesis 3:15). The tyranny of death over man is broken by Christ's death and resurrection. It is interesting to note that Christ uses death to defeat death – a point often made during this period by preachers. An appeal was often made to the story of David and Goliath – just as David killed Goliath with the giant's own weapon, so Christ defeated death with its own weapons.

The idea of Christ 'wakening the imprisoned dead' reflects the belief that Christ's death and resurrection were important, not only for those alive at the time and in years to come, but also for those who had come before. The basic idea is that Christ's victory over death is retrospective as well as prospective, and is thus good news for those who have already died. These are understood to be prisoners held captive by death, and through the defeat of death by Christ they are delivered from their bondage and set free. In the Middle Ages, this idea was developed as the 'harrowing of hell' – an interesting idea worth looking at briefly.

The idea of the harrowing of hell is loosely based upon some New Testament passages which could be interpreted as suggesting that Christ went down to the place of the departed – in other words, hell – between his crucifixion and resurrection (Matthew 12:39–40; Acts 2:27–31; Romans 10:7; Colossians 1:18; and especially 1 Peter 3:18–22). The basic idea is that Christ descended into hell, with the cross of victory, and took the castle of hell by storm, setting free all those held prisoner. In the great portrayals of this scene dating from the fourteenth century, Christ tends to appear like a medieval knight, using his cross as a lance to break down the castle doors. But perhaps the most familiar portrayal of this powerful image for the modern reader is to be found in the religious allegory *The Lion, the Witch and the Wardrobe* by C. S. Lewis.

In this work we encounter the White Witch who keeps the land of Narnia covered in wintry snow. In the midst of this land of winter stands the witch's castle, within which many of the inhabitants of Narnia have been imprisoned as stone statues. In the fourteenth chapter of the book, Lewis describes the killing of Aslan, perhaps the most demonic episode ever to have found its way into a children's story. The forces of darkness and oppression seem to have won a terrible victory – and yet, in that victory lies their defeat. Aslan surrenders himself to the forces of evil, and allows them to do their worst with him – and by doing so, disarms them. In the famous words of William Cullen Bryant, 'Truth crushed to earth will rise again.' The description of the resurrection of Aslan is one the book's more tender moments, evoking the deep sense of sorrow so evident in the New Testament accounts of the burial of Christ, and the joy of recognition of the reality of the resurrection. In the sixteenth chapter of the book, Lewis graphically describes how Aslan – the lion of Judah, who has burst his chains – breaks into the castle, breathes upon the statues and restores them to life, before leading the liberated army through the shattered gates of the once-great fortress to freedom. Hell has been harrowed – it has been despoiled and its inhabitants liberated from its dreary shades.

It will, however, be obvious that the struggle between good and evil continues to this day. So how can we talk about the cross as a decisive victory over evil? The crucifixion and resurrection are seen by the New Testament writers as a turning point, a decisive battle, in God's war against the evil powers that enslave and incapacitate man. This war was not begun with the birth of Christ, nor was it ended with his resurrection. The war has been going on since the beginning of time, and continues to this day. But the death and resurrection of Christ mark the dawn of a new and a decisive phase in this struggle, in which victory has been gained and yet not gained. To illustrate this point, let us consider a modern example.

On a fateful day in June 1944, the Allied forces managed to establish a bridgehead in Europe on the beaches of Normandy. This momentous day was called 'D-Day', and historians have emphasized that it marked a decisive turning point in the history of the Second World War. The war was not won on that day – victory did not come until the following year, on 'VE-Day'. But, in a sense, the war *was* won on that day – because from that moment onwards, the war entered a new phase, a phase of victory. Looking back on the history of the Second World War, the great turning point may be identified as the seizing of a bridgehead, a small pocket of Allied land in the midst of hostile territory, in June 1944.

So it is with the incarnation, death and resurrection of Jesus Christ. In the incarnation, God established a bridgehead in hostile territory from which to begin the reconquest of his own world. In Christ's death and resurrection, we may see the age-old conflict between good and evil entering a new phase. It has not yet been won, but it is as if we have been granted a preview of the end of history, and can know that, in the end, evil will be destroyed. And from that standpoint, the cross and resurrection are seen as the turning point, the moment in which victory was gained and yet not gained. The cross and resurrection are to D-Day as the end of history is to VE-Day. We know that sin and death are defeated, even if the battle goes on around us.

A final point may be considered. Does not the emphasis upon the victory given in the cross diminish the place of the suffering of Christ in obtaining this victory? That this is a real danger may readily be conceded – but it is easily avoided. One of the most powerful pieces of reflection upon the meaning of the cross was written before 750 in Old English, and is widely known as the *Dream of the Rood* ('Rood' is the Old English, or Anglo-Saxon, word for 'cross'). In this poem, the writer tells of how he dreamed 'the best of dreams', in which he saw a cross studded with the jewels and richness of victory:

> It was as though I saw a wondrous tree
> Towering in the sky, diffused with light.

Yet as he wonders at this 'glorious tree of victory', it changes its appearance before his eyes, becoming covered with blood and gore. How can it be that this strange tree should have two so very different appearances? As he wonders, the cross begins to speak for itself, telling him its story. It tells of how it was once a young tree, growing in a forest, only to be chopped down and taken to a hill. When it had been firmly put in its place, a hero came and voluntarily mounted it:

> Then the young hero (who was God almighty)
> Got ready, resolute, and strong in heart.
> He climbed onto the lofty gallows-tree,
> Bold in the sight of all who watched,
> For he intended to redeem mankind.

Before his eyes, the young hero is pierced with dark nails. The tree is penetrated by those same nails and drenched with the blood which pours from their wounds – and yet it is through this appalling suffering that victory is gained and man set free. And so the poet tries to show how the gloriously jewelled cross of victory – perhaps an allusion to the crosses carried in processions in churches at the time – is actually pierced with nails and drenched with blood. Christ suffered on the 'gallows-tree', and yet was 'successful and victorious' in his mission. The cost of this victory was high and must never be forgotten:

> May God be friend to me
> He who suffered once upon the gallows-tree
> Here on earth for men's sins. He redeemed us
> And granted us our life and heavenly home.

And if this seems to amount to triumphalism, it must be remembered that the victory won is not that of force but of tenderness: the symbol of victory, which goes forth conquering and to conquer, is the figure of a lamb as if it had been slain.

Why is this theme of the divine victory over sin, death and evil so important? Perhaps the most convincing answer to this question is given by Martin Luther King in his famous sermon *The Death of Evil upon the Seashore* (the title of the sermon derives from Exodus 14:30: 'And Israel saw the Egyptians dead upon the sea shore'). The belief that God has already entered into battle with the forces of evil gives hope to man as he attempts to wrestle with evil in his own day. As we struggle to defeat the forces of evil, we know that God is struggling with us. At the very moment when evil seems to gain its greatest victory, it is defeated with its own weapons. The faith that God has entered into man's conflict against his enemies, on his side, sustains him in his struggle to escape from the bondage of every evil Egypt. The great theme of 'the victorious God' gives hope where otherwise there would be despair, and sustains man in his endless, and seemingly unwinnable, fight against evil. The darkness and despair of Good Friday must give way to the triumph of Easter Day. As Martin Luther King so wisely observed, 'without such faith, man's highest dreams will pass silently to the dust.'

11

The Forgiving God

The great theme of a God who forgives his wayward people
is touchingly portrayed in the parable of the prodigal son.
The waiting father, as we have seen, rushes out to greet the
returning son and forgive him for his waywardness. The
parable draws our attention to the love of the father for his
son. It also, however, raises a question for many people:
how can the father just forgive the son like that? It seems
rather superficial, almost as if the father is suggesting that
the past may be forgotten, set aside as if it never happened.
Our sympathies often actually lie with the second son who is
outraged by his father's behaviour!

It is, however, unfair to expect a single parable to bring
out the many aspects of the Christian understanding of the
nature of forgiveness. This particular parable focusses our
attention upon the love of the father. Parables usually just
make one point, and the point which this parable makes is
that a loving God eagerly awaits the return of his wayward
children. This is one aspect of the Christian understanding of
God, but it is quite ridiculous to suppose that this is all that
there is to it. It is an insight which is to be treasured, to be
sure, but it is by no means all that has to be said about God.
It is quite improper to single out this parable as if it presented the gospel in a nutshell, as if we could dispense
with the remainder of the New Testament. There are many

passages in the New Testament which draw attention to the seriousness with which God takes sin, and the great cost of true forgiveness.

The Lord's Prayer draws a direct comparison between God's forgiveness of our sins and our forgiveness of other people's sins (Matthew 6:12, 14–15), and makes it clear that if we don't forgive the sins of others, God won't forgive ours. Yet we all know from our own experience, only too painfully, how very difficult it is to forgive someone. It is easy to forgive someone for something unimportant, but when it is something really important, something which means a lot to us, we find it very difficult. It is here that the difference between real and false forgiveness becomes clear. It is very easy to say 'I forgive you', to someone who has deeply hurt us, and not mean it. Resentment against that person remains, and we have 'forgiven' them in word only and not in reality. Real forgiveness means confronting the hurt which has been caused, recognizing its full extent and importance. It means going to the person who has caused such hurt and pain, and explaining the situation to him. It means telling him that, despite the great hurt and injury which has been done, his continued friendship is of such importance that you want him to accept your offer of forgiveness. And that is a difficult offer to accept – because it involves a deeply humbling admisssion, that injury has been caused. It may even be that we are unaware of the hurt and pain we cause to those whom we love by our actions. Forgiveness is an essential aspect of human personal relationships, such as love and trust. Without real forgiveness, our relationships with others would be false and superficial.

So it is with our relationship with God. The cross brings home to us the deep hurt and pain which our sin causes God. In Christ, God makes clear how painful and costly true forgiveness really is. And it is a real forgiveness which God offers us in Christ – a forgiveness which, if accepted, will transform our relationship with God. The offer of forgiveness of our sins is both deeply humiliating and deeply satisfying. It is humiliating because it forces us to recognize and acknowledge our sin; it is satisfying because the very offer of forgiveness implies that God treats us as important to him. God offers us forgiveness because, despite our sin, he loves us and wants us to return to him, to relate to him as we are meant to. God created us in his image and likeness (Genesis 1:26–27), thus we have an inbuilt capacity to relate to God which sin threatens to frustrate and which forgiveness offers to restore.

The theme of the 'image of God in man' is an important one and worth thinking about a little more. When I was at school, we used to enjoy playing around with chemicals in the school laboratory. One of the more amusing tricks was to get a really old copper coin and drop it in a beaker of dilute nitric acid. The acid would turn blue and rather unpleasant brown fumes would be given off – and the coin would appear as if it were new. The acid had dissolved the dirt and grime which had obscured the features of the coin. The interesting point is this: the coins we used for this experiment were old British pennies which had the image of Queen Victoria stamped upon them. This image would, however, be quite invisible on account of the accumulated dirt. Although the image was there, it could not be seen. The acid restored the image so that it was clearly visible. Christianity has always insisted that although the image of God in man is obscured and hidden through sin, it remains there nevertheless. It just needs something to restore it – a theological equivalent of dilute nitric acid, in fact. The gospel could be seen as restoring the image of God, man's ability to relate to God, by removing the obstacles to this relationship. Forgiveness does not necessarily mean that *sin* is eliminated – it means that the *threat sin poses to man's relationship to God* is eliminated. There is all the difference in the world between being sinless and being forgiven!

So far, however, we have just been talking about personal relationships. What about the wider consequences of forgiveness? What about its effect upon a group of people, upon the community? The distinction that we are about to draw is well known, and in English law is summed up in the difference between a *tort* and a *crime*. A tort is a personal injury, something which somebody does to me (like being rude to me in the absence of witnesses) which has no effect on anyone else and which I can forgive without involving anyone else. A crime is something which someone does to me (like robbing me or murdering me) which has wider effects upon the community. Robbing and murdering injure the community and not just me as an individual – and as a result, have to be dealt with by the community. If anyone can be said to 'forgive' these actions, it is the community against which they have been committed, and not just me as an individual. And it is here that we are forced to recognize that human sin has consequences not just for the relationship of an individual with God, but for the relationship of people in general. This point is particularly clear in the Old Testament, where the destructive effects of sin upon the community of Israel are emphasized. Sin is about self-centredness (how often it has been pointed out that the centre of 'sin' is 'I'), which means that we ignore both God and our neighbour in our actions. The impact of sin is felt at both the private and the communal level. The question of how God can forgive sin thus comes to concern the *justice* of this forgiveness. How can God forgive sin when it has such consequences for society? Will this forgiveness not encourage man to commit sin?

The legal thory of the atonement attempts to meet these objections by demonstrating that God acts in complete justice in forgiving sin through the death of Christ. Although the roots of this idea are deeply embedded in both the Old and New Testaments, the first systematic development of the theory is to be found in the works of Anselm, the eleventh-century Archbishop of Canterbury. This idea has since become so influential that it is worth examining in some detail.

Anselm expresses his dissatisfaction with the understanding of the death of Christ as a victory over sin, death and evil, because it does not really explain why Christ is involved in this victory in the first place. Why could God not have gained this great victory in some other way? How does Christ's death come into the picture? Anselm therefore sets out to develop a theory of the meaning of the death of Christ which firmly established its necessity as the means by which God worked out the salvation of the world.

His argument goes like this. God make mankind in order that he might have eternal life, but unfortunately man's sin intervened to make it impossible for him to gain eternal life unaided. So if man is going to have eternal life, God will have to do something about it. God cannot just pretend that sin doesn't exist or dismiss it as unimportant. Anselm then draws an analogy from the feudal outlook of the period. In ordinary life, an offence against a person can be forgiven, provided that some sort of compensation is given for the offence. Anselm refers to this compensation as a 'satisfaction'. For example, a man might steal a sum of money from his neighbour: in order to meet the demands of justice, he would have to restore that sum of money, plus an additional sum for the offence given by the theft in the first place – and this additional sum of money is the 'satisfaction'. Anselm then argues that sin is an offence against God, for which a satisfaction is required. As God is infinite, an infinite satisfaction is required. But as man is finite, he can't pay this satisfaction. And so it seems impossible that man shall ever have his eternal life.

Anselm then makes the following point. Although man ought to pay the satisfaction, he cannot; and although God is under no obligation to pay the satisfaction, he clearly could if he wanted to. And so, Anselm argues, it is quite clear that a

God-man would be both able and obliged to pay this satisfaction. Therefore, he argues, the incarnation and death of Jesus Christ may be seen as a means of resolving this dilemma. As man, Christ has an obligation to pay the satisfaction; as God, he has the ability to pay it. And so the satisfaction is paid off, and man is able to regain eternal life.

Anselm's theory was important because it showed that a good case could be made for involving the death of Christ in the scheme of the divine forgiveness of sin without contravening justice. The theory has, of course, been very heavily criticized – for example, on account of its feudal ideas. But Anselm was just doing what every good preacher tries to do – use contemporary analogies to make a theological point. In a feudal society, like Anselm's, you would use feudal analogies. We can hardly expect him to have imagined what life would have been like in the sixteenth or twentieth centuries! The basic point which Anselm made is still of crucial importance – and that is that God does not act in an arbitrary or unjust way in redeeming mankind, but is totally faithful to his righteousness. God is not involved in questionable actions (like deceiving the devil) nor does he pretend that sin is insignificant and can be overlooked. For Anselm, God is just and acts in accordance with that justice in redeeming mankind. It is this authentic New Testament insight which Anselm has so vigorously upheld, even if his defence of the insight takes him far from the cautious statements of the New Testament on the matter.

A useful distinction which may be made here is between 'justice' or 'law', and 'laws'. The words 'law' or 'justice' express the basic principle of not acting arbitrarily but in accordance with generally accepted standards, whereas 'laws' are various expressions of what those standards might be. Thus practically everyone agrees that 'law' is a good thing, but when it comes to defining what it means, disagreement arises. 'Law' is recognized as essential, while the 'laws' which express it are a matter for debate. Thus Anselm justifies the idea of redemption by *law* by an appeal to eleventh-century *laws*, just as Calvin made an appeal to sixteenth-century laws – but the fact that those laws no longer apply today doesn't actually invalidate the basic principle he is trying to establish. The legal approach to the death of Christ is concerned with *law*, rather than with *laws* – in other words, with the basic conviction that God acts justly in dealing with sin and redeeming mankind. The cross demonstrates that the guilt of sin is really forgiven, and makes clear the full cost of this forgiveness.

The New Testament itself is not particularly concerned with the mechanics of the death of Christ – how it is that God is able to forgive the sins of man through the death of Christ. Of course, by drawing analogies with the Old Testament sacrificial system and the Suffering Servant of Isaiah 53, it gives us hints about ways in which we might relate Christ's death to our forgiveness, and these hints have been developed in the various legal theories of the atonement. All these theories make the same point expressed so simply by Mrs Cecil F. Alexander:

> There was no other good enough
> To pay the price of sin;
> He only could unlock the gate
> Of heaven, and let us in.

But the New Testament's real concern lies elsewhere – in the emphatic assertion and proclamation that God really has dealt justly with human sin through the cross of Christ. It was through the cross of Christ, and through this alone, that real forgiveness of real sins became possible. How this was done is of relatively little importance in comparison with the fact that it was done. The guilt and the power of sin were broken through Christ. But it is worth noticing that the New Testament does not portray God as a cruel tyrant who arbitrarily demands the suffering and death of an innocent victim in order that the guilty party may escape his anger. The idea of a bloodthirsty, vengeful God has no place at all in the New Testament, which affirms that God himself entered into history in order to suffer for offending sinners. If *anyone* suffers, it is God himself who suffers on man's behalf and in man's place in order that justice and mercy might both be satisfied. It is the judge himself who suffers in order that his own law may be upheld and man truly and justly forgiven.

Forgiveness, then, if it is to be real forgiveness, is a costly business. Just how much it costs God to forgive man his sin is shown in the cross – the torment of the dying Christ, the incarnate God, gives us a most vivid and distressing insight into the nature and extent of God's forgiving love. As the *Dream of the Rood* puts it so powerfully:

> This is the tree of glory
> On which God Almighty once suffered torment
> For the many sins of mankind, and for the deeds
> Of Adam long ago.

It is God who suffers in order to bring home to man how precious real forgiveness can be. And although forgiveness is a difficult offer to accept because of the clear implication that we are at fault, the thought of the crucified God makes this an offer we may find easier to accept than might otherwise be the case. The love and compassion shown in God's forgiveness make the gentle chiding of our faithlessness more bearable. Christ is the only man in history to see sin through the eyes of God, to see sin for what it really is. And in the crucifixion we are shown the full horror of the consequences of sin, and the urgency of the call to repent, to turn away from it to the one who alone may break its hold upon us. The cross reveals both the seriousness of sin, and the purpose and power of God to overcome it.

How, then, are we involved in this process of forgiveness? Three main ways of dealing with this question have been suggested. The first is that of substitution – Christ, the righteous man, takes our place on the cross. It is we who should have been crucified, yet Christ took our place, removing from us the penalties due for sin. This idea is suggested by several passages in the New Testament. 'For our sake he [God] made him [Christ] to be sin who knew no sin, so that in him we might become the righteousness of God' (2 Corinthians 5:21). The second is that of participation – man participates in the forgiveness which Christ won upon the cross. This view draws upon many New Testament passages, particularly Romans 8, in which the constant involvement of the believer with all that Christ has done is constantly emphasized. The believer participates in whatever Christ has done: we share in Christ's suffering, death and final glorification. The third is that of representation – Christ represents man to God, just as he represents God to man. And as the representative of man, Christ wins forgiveness for him on his behalf. Christ is thus understood to suffer on the cross on behalf of, but not instead of, sinful man. But whichever of these models the reader finds most helpful in dealing with the New Testament statements on the involvement of the believer in the death and resurrection of Christ, the fact that he *is* understood to be involved in some way is not questioned. In some way, each of us may be said to have been present at Christ's crucifixion, just as in some way, each of us may be said to share in his resurrection.

Why is the idea of forgiveness so important? Man needs to know that, despite his sin, he may enter into fellowship with God. One of the most remarkable features of the gospel is the assertion that man is brought to God through God being brought to man. There are many religions which teach that God does not welcome man until he ceases being a sinner – in other words, man must become righteous before he can enter into fellowship with God. God in Christ first welcomes man, and in that way brings about a *real* transformation in man. Forgiveness imparts, rather than demands, newness of life. It is the offer of forgiveness, so powerfully and tenderly embodied in the dying incarnate God, Jesus Christ, which

brings home to man his need for repentance and amend-
ment. Man can come to God, just as he is, knowing that the
offer of pardon and forgiveness carries with it the promise of
transformation and renewal:

> Just as I am, without one plea
> But that Thy blood was shed for me,
> And that Thou bidst me come to Thee,
> O Lamb of God, I come.

PART 4
Conclusion

12

The Identity and Significance of Jesus Christ

Who is Jesus Christ? And why is he so important for Christians? These are the questions which have dominated this book. As we emphasized at the beginning, there is a very close connection between the person and the work of Jesus Christ – between who Jesus is and what he did. Although we have actually been more interested in the question of the identity of Jesus, we have also tried to show some of the ways in which Christians have understood the meaning of Christ's death. In the late seventeenth century, Isaac Newton discovered that a beam of white light, when passed through a glass prism, was split into a beam containing all the colours of the rainbow. The prism didn't create those colours – they had always been there in the beam of light – it just enabled them to be separated from each other and seen individually. Much the same sort of process leads to the formation of a rainbow, with raindrops acting as prisms. And so it is with our reflections on Jesus Christ. Just as the prism showed up the many components of a beam of white light, so we have tried to show the many ideas and insights which are contained in the death and resurrection of Jesus Christ, and look at them individually. They haven't been invented – just uncovered. But in the end we must remember that they are all part and parcel of one and the same thing – the person of Jesus Christ.

The cross is the central symbol of the Christian faith. It is the sign which is made at our baptism, when we bind ourselves to the God and Father of our Lord Jesus Christ. It is the sign which adorns our churches. It was in this sign that the first Christian Roman Emperor, Constantine, went forth to conquer. As we have seen in this work, it is the cross which establishes the distinctively Christian understanding of the nature of God, and brings home to us with some force the full implications of God's love and forgiveness. The identity and significance of Jesus Christ are fully disclosed through the cross – first by his being crucified upon it, and then by his being raised from the death which it brought. The empty cross, as much as the empty tomb, reminds us of the strange and mysterious way in which God is at work in the world. To end this book, we are going to bring together some of the thoughts which have been developed here and which have relevance to both the individual believer, as he attempts to understand his own faith better and explain it to others, and to the life of the Christian church in general.

Let us begin by looking at the relevance of what has been said so far to the individual believer. The impact and relevance of the cross could be summarized very simply in four familiar images or pictures which help illustrate the meaning of the cross and draw on ideas we have already discussed. There is much more that could be said about the cross, as we have tried to show, and it could be said a lot better and more profoundly than this – but these four points should be helpful as 'discussion starters'. The reader who has had any difficulty in following the discussion in the earlier part of this book may find it helpful to treat them as 'pegs' on which to hang the various points we have been making.

1. The cross as the place where God and man meet

Imagine that you are driving along a country road, perhaps at night. As you drive along, your headlights pick up a sign at the side of the road. It has a cross on it. What does it mean? It means that there is a crossroads ahead, and that means oncoming traffic. Unless you are careful, you may find yourself in collision with another vehicle. The cross here means 'a point of meeting'. And so it is with the cross of Christ. God and man meet in the cross. It is through the cross that God discloses himself to us, calls to us and meets us. Christianity is about coming to the foot of the cross, recognizing that in some strange and mysterious way the same God who made heaven and earth makes himself available for us at this very place. In the cross and resurrection of Jesus we recognize that Jesus is none other than God himself, humbling himself, even to death on a cross in order to bring us home from the far country.

Let us remember once more that very powerful parable of the prodigal son. It is a very moving and vivid illustration of the love of the father for his wayward son. Perhaps the thought of Jesus dying on the cross suggests that we might develop this parable slightly to bring out the full-blooded meaning of the death of Christ: the father goes after the son into the far country and brings him home, despite the appalling cost of this venture to himself. It is God who comes to meet us, who searches us out and finds us, to bring us home to him. In that dreadful image of the dying crucified Christ, we are presented with the sight of God, raised up high upon the cross, drawing men to himself. 'Behold, my servant . . . shall be exalted and lifted up' (Isaiah 52:13) – only now do we realize the full significance of those prophetic remarks. The servant was indeed exalted and lifted up – not exalted in status, by being made a king, but by being exalted and raised up upon the cross in order that all men might see and wonder (John 3:14–15; 12:32–33).

2. The cross as the demonstration of man's sin

Now imagine that you are back at school. You are doing some arithmetic – a very simple sum:

$$5 + 7 = ?$$

is the problem you have to solve. After much thought (remember, you're very young again!) you write the answer with a flourish:

$$5 + 7 = 13$$

and the teacher promptly scrawls a symbol by the sum to show that you are wrong – a cross. A cross means wrong, not right. In a similar way, the cross means that we are not right with God. It tells us that we are sinners, men and women who need his grace and forgiveness. Can you see what a costly thing forgiveness is for God? God is loving, as we have seen, but he is also holy and righteous. How, then, can he *really* forgive us sinners? He can't just say, 'Never mind, we'll pretend it never happened' – even we couldn't accept that idea of forgiveness. In the cross of Christ, we are talking about the *real* forgiveness of *real* sins, not some sort of pretend, fairy-tale stuff. God's forgiveness of sin comes about through the death of Christ on the cross – *real* forgiveness of *real* sin – in which we come face to face with both God's total condemnation of sin and his incredible and overwhelming love for us sinners:

> We may not know, we cannot tell,
> What pains He had to bear;
> But we believe it was for us,
> He hung and suffered there.

Christ died upon the cross to take upon himself our sin. Through his suffering and death upon the cross, perhaps in a way we shall never understand, God was able to forgive our sin. This astonishing fact should make us get down on our

it. The first step in the process of healing is identifying what
the problem is. And so it is with judgement passed upon us
in the cross of Christ – a judgement which identifies that
something is wrong with man and thus opens the way to
healing, transformation and renewal. The idea of Christ as
the 'light of the world' (John 8:12) is useful here – light
shows up things for what they really are, bringing everything
to light and making clear the dilemma with which man is
faced. Perhaps we could say that the cross offers a diagnosis
of the human situation as the first step towards transforming
it.

3. The cross as the demonstration of God's love

Imagine that you are writing a letter to someone very dear to
you. Perhaps you are sending a Valentine card or a very
personal letter. You write it, sign it and then indicate your
affection for the person who will receive the letter by placing
crosses at the bottom. Crosses mean love. The cross brings
home to us the full extent of God's love for his people. 'God
so loved the world that he gave his only Son' (John 3:16).
'God shows his love for us in that while we were yet sinners
Christ died for us' (Romans 5:8).

It is an astonishing thought that God – when the full meaning of this word is grasped – actually loves us personally. It
seems strange and impossible. There is simply no limit to the
love of God for us. As Christ was dying upon the cross, those
around him made fun of him. 'Come down from the cross,'
they screamed. 'Save yourself!' But he didn't – he stayed
where he was and died, showing that there was no limit to his
love for us. There was simply nothing more that could be
given than his own life. 'Save yourself,' the crowd shouted,
and yet Jesus died in order to save us instead. The words of a
famous Christmas hymn are enlightening here:

> O may we keep and ponder in our mind
> God's wondrous love in saving lost mankind.

knees in wonder, rather than rush to speculate about th
mechanics of the process!

The gospel tells us that we are far from God, lost in a dar
world and desperately needing hope, meaning and love. The
feeling of 'lostness' might make us wonder if there is, in fact
anyone who is ever going to meet us and find us. The cross of
Christ tells us that, even though we are sinners, God has not
forsaken us but has taken the initiative in meeting us and
finding us. Christ's suffering and death upon the cross were
for us – he died to show us how far we are from God and at
the same time to open the way back to God. The cross
exposes sin and shows how its power and guilt can be broken.
The cross stands at the centre of the Christian faith, revealing
both the seriousness of human sin and the purpose and power
of God to deal with it. If you think of sin as guilt, think of
Christ as bearing our sin upon the cross; if you think of sin as
despair, reflect upon the hope we have set before us in Christ's
victory over death; if you think of sin as being far from God,
rejoice in the fact that God has met us in Christ and offered to
bring us home. Jesus said, 'I am the way, and the truth, and the
life' (John 14:6). He did not merely show us the way and then
leave us to make our journey unaided. Like the shepherd, he
guides us along that way, travelling with us (Psalm 23 is worth
reading again in this connection).

The cross, then, brings judgement – but we must not think of
this judgement as something that is purely negative in which
God just blames us or shows up how inadequate we are for the
fun of it. Perhaps another everyday situation in which judgement is given may help bring this point out. When a doctor
diagnoses an illness, he is passing a judgement on you – he is
telling you what is wrong with you. But he is telling you what is
wrong with you in order that you may be cured. And in order
to be cured, you need to know what is wrong with you. It is
remarkable how many people who are ill are quite unaware of
the fact – they just accept their situation as normal, unaware
that something is wrong and that something can be done about

> Trace we the Babe, who hath retrieved our loss,
> From his poor manger to his bitter cross;
> Tread in his steps, assisted by his grace,
> Till man's first heavenly state again takes place.

God, in his tender mercy, set forth on the humiliating and costly journey to the far country to meet his lost children and bring them home. Like the good shepherd, he was prepared to lay down his life for his sheep (John 10:11).

4. The cross as a decision

Let us now turn to a fourth way in which we might use a cross in everyday life. Placing a cross against a name on a ballot paper means you are voting for them; it means that you are making a decision. The cross of Jesus Christ also demands a decision. As we have seen, God offers man love, forgiveness and reconciliation through the cross. And this offer forces us to make a decision: will we respond to it or not? Forgiveness or reconciliation offered and not accepted does not transform a relationship. In effect, God has given us the immense privilege of saying 'No' to his offer of love. He knocks on the door, gently, seeking admission (Revelation 3:20–21) but we must open the door. A favourite analogy for this in the Middle Ages was the opening of a shutter. Let us suppose that you are in a dark room and want it lit up. The shutter is closed and the sunlight is beaming down upon that shutter, yet the light will not enter that room and illuminate it until you open that shutter. So it is with the forgiving grace of God – like the sunlight, it is always there at our disposal. But a decision, an action, is required if it is to influence us or affect us. Opening that shutter to let the light in is just like saying 'Yes' to God's offer of grace.

A famous German poem by Angelus Silesius has been quoted much in the present century by theologians. The important lines go like this:

Were Christ a thousand times to Bethlehem come,
And yet not born in you, it would spell your doom.
Golgotha's cross, it cannot save from sin,
Unless for you that cross is raised within.
I say, it helps you not that Christ is risen,
If you yourself are still in death's dark prison.

In other words, the incarnation, crucifixion and resurrection are of little relevance to anyone unless they are received and appropriated by faith. Christ was born in Bethlehem, but he must be born in *us* if he is to do us any good. Christ died on the cross of Calvary, but unless we make that cross our own, unless we accept and receive its power by faith, it remains a distant, remote and not particularly relevant event. The great gap of space and time which separates us from the death and resurrection of Jesus Christ is bridged by faith in order to grasp and appropriate what is on offer. Faith, to use John Calvin's famous analogy, is like an empty, open hand stretched out towards God, with nothing to offer and everything to receive. Faith is the final step in the process begun by the cross of Christ – we recognize its meaning, we realize its relevance and finally we receive its benefits.

The cross, then, is central to the faith of the individual believer. Like John Bunyan's *Pilgrim*, he may lay his burdens at its foot and go forward into a new life. But an important part of that new life is the community of faith, the Christian church, which has been called out from the world as the people of God. What is the relevance of the cross to that church?

First, the cross must be allowed to function as the foundation and the criterion of the church's understanding of its identity and its mission. It is through the strange and mysterious events which culminate in the crucifixion and resurrection of her Lord that she came into being, and it is recalled, rehearsed and re-enacted in the service variously known as the eucharist, communion or breaking of bread. Here the church is reminded of something which she must never be allowed to forget – that whatever social, political or cultural situation she may find herself in, her distinctive identity lies in the fact that she has been called from the world by the series of events leading up to and then away from the cross. It is the 'word of the cross' which she must proclaim and by which she must judge first herself and then others. The essential and vital *distinctiveness* of Christianity can all too easily be lost: all that then remains is a church which retains its structure but has lost both meaning and experience. In an age where society has taken over most of the social functions once exercized by the church, there is an increasingly urgent need for that church to rediscover the vitality and authenticity of the original function of the church – there is no sadder sight than a church seeking for a meaning which was once given to it and which it has now lost.

In the light of the cross, and the grim spectacle of the crucified Christ, we realize the futility of the world's values and ideals. In the famous words of Thomas à Kempis, 'The glory of the world fades away' (*sic transit gloria mundi*). In the eyes of the world, 'might is right' – but the church must learn to conquer in weakness. The sign in which she will conquer is that of a lamb who has been slain. Yet in her weakness lies her greatest strength. The dying Christ who, counter to every expectation was raised from death in power and glory, is the model by which the church must gain and exercise authority. There is no room for triumphalism or self-confidence: simply a recognition of the need to return continually to the foot of the cross, there to reflect upon the mysterious way in which God works in his world and in his church. Perhaps it is significant that the church tends to be at its weakest spiritually when it possesses its greatest temporal strength. In the eyes of the world, a system of beliefs must be sophisticated and subtle if it is ever to gain acceptance, but the church must learn that her only wisdom is the foolishness of the cross and the proclamation of Christ crucified. This proclamation seems hopelessly weak and foolish, and there is every temptation to embellish it with what our day and age accepts as wisdom – yet which another generation will regard as discredited. In the cross, we are confronted with a set of values different from those of the world – what the world sees as folly and weakness and humiliation is recognized by those with the insight of faith as the wisdom and the strength and the glory of the living God (1 Corinthians 1:17–31). The passionate concern of the Christian and the church for the affairs of the world in which they live must be accompanied by a critical attitude towards its standards, expectations and hopes.

We must also note a temptation to which the church is prone to in her preaching and her reflection upon the gospel message which has been entrusted to her. That temptation is to treat Christianity as primarily a set of interesting moral or religious *ideas* which can be conveyed by teaching or argument. Unfortunately, people cannot be argued into the kingdom of God, because what is entrusted to the church is not so much a set of ideas as the living reality which lies behind them. It is the crucified and risen Christ who stands at the centre of the Christian faith – a *person*, not a set of *ideas*.

There is a story which is told (in a number of versions!) about the philosopher Bertrand Russell. One day, he was walking down a road when he suddenly stopped and said to himself, 'The ontological argument is right after all!' (In other words, that a certain philosophical proof for the existence of God was valid.) On another day, somewhat earlier in human history, Saul of Tarsus was walking down a different road when he encountered the risen Christ. Russell had encountered an idea; Saul had met a person – and there is all the difference in the world between the two experiences. That encounter with the risen Christ certainly gave rise to a set of ideas – but lying behind them as their source and origin was the risen Christ. We are often told that faith is 'caught, not taught', and the point which this statement makes is simply that there is far more to Christianity than a set of ideas, rules or beliefs, and that assent to these isn't the same as the experience of encountering Jesus Christ. The cross reminds us that the central question we were once forced to ask ourselves, and which we must subsequently force others to ask, is not, 'Do you believe *this* idea or *that* idea?' but, 'Who do *you* say Jesus Christ is?'

In this book we have been concerned with exploring the various ways of understanding the full significance of Jesus Christ and his relevance for us. There are many matters which have been discussed all too briefly, and an embarrassingly large number of questions which haven't been discussed at all! It is, however, hoped that this book will stimulate its readers to begin to think further for themselves on the full relevance of Jesus Christ. But now we must conclude.

The 'word of the cross' (1 Corinthians 1:18) is the story of a God who loved his wayward children to the point where he stooped down from heaven to meet them and suffered and died upon the cross to demonstrate the full extent of his overwhelming compassion and care for those whom he loved. God journeyed into the far country, enduring its suffering, pain and agony, to meet us and embrace us. Like a great beacon, the cross stands as a sign summoning men to discover the 'God and Father of our Lord Jesus Christ', the God of the cross, who counted us worthy of so great a sacrifice. Why should God love sinful man? Why did the cross have to happen? In the end, these questions are not terribly important. The important point is that the cross did happen, and that 'the word of the cross' is that, astonishing and incredible though it may seem, God loves us and gives himself for us. Like a beacon on a hill, the cross stands as a symbol of hope in despair, life in the midst of death, light in the darkness. 'When I am lifted up, I will draw all men to myself' (John 12:32). Then, as now, the cross is charged with the power, love and compassion of God. It is the bread of life waiting to satisfy the hunger of men. In the words of Thomas à Kempis:

> There is no salvation of soul, no hope of eternal life, except in the cross. Therefore, take up the cross, and go forward into eternal life. Christ has gone there before you, bearing his cross. He died for you upon the cross, that you may bear your cross, and die on the cross with him. For if you die with him, you will live with him; if you share his sufferings, you will share his glory.

Through the cross, God meets us in our lostness and finds us, setting us on the road which leads home – a road on which Christ has gone before us, blazing a trail in which we may follow, knowing that by doing so, we pass from death to eternal life.